the Catholic Church and the American Poor

the Catholic Church and the American Poor

George A. Kelly

Theodore Lownik Library
Illinois Benedictine College
Lisle, IL 60532

ALBA · HOUSE NEW · YORK

SOCIETY OF ST. PAUL, 2187 VICTORY BLVD., STATEN ISLAND, NEW YORK 10314

BV
639
.P6
K42
1976

*Library of Congress Cataloging
in Publication Data*

Kelley, George Anthony, 1916-
The Catholic Church and
the American poor.

Includes bibliographical references.
1. Church and the poor.
2. Poor-United States.
3. Church and social problems—
Catholic Church. I. Title.
BV639.P6K42 261.'8'34'41 75-16293
ISBN 0-8189-0321-X

Nihil Obstat:
Daniel V. Flynn, J.C.D.
Censor Librorum

Imprimatur:
+ James P. Mahoney, D.D.
Vicar General, Archdiocese of New York
May 14, 1975

*The Nihil Obstat and Imprimatur
are a declaration that a book or pamphlet is considered
to be free from doctrinal or moral error. It is not implied that
those who have granted the Nihil Obstat and Imprimatur agree
with the contents, opinions or statements expressed.*

*Designed, printed and bound in the United States of
America by the Fathers and Brothers of the Society of St. Paul,
2187 Victory Boulevard, Staten Island, New York, 10314,
as part of their communications apostolate.*

1 2 3 4 5 6 7 8 9 (Current Printing: first digit).

© *Copyright 1976 by the Society of St. Paul*

dedicated to

MSGR. PAUL HANLY FURFEY
BISHOP FRANCIS J. HAAS
MSGR. JOHN P. MONAGHAN
FR. WILFRED PARSONS, S.J.
MSGR. JOHN A. RYAN

Who on behalf of the Church were working for the poor long before the rest of us knew there really was a problem.

INTRODUCTION

My introduction in 1942 to the social doctrine of the Church
came through the good offices of John P. Monaghan, Francis J.
Haas, Paul Hanly Furfey, Wilfred Parsons, S.J., and John A. Ryan
in that order. There was some elementary connection with the
papal social encyclicals during seminary days of the 1930's.
Charles E. Coughlin and Fulton J. Sheen in different ways and
with different results were Catholic batters in a public arena where
Pro-New Dealers and Anti-New Dealers bludgeoned each other.
Those who were involved with Frank Sheed's *Catholic Evidence
Guild,* often drafted by that saintly Jesuit Francis Le Buffe, were
forced by the circumstances of debating Communists on Columbus
Circle or Union Square to acquaint themselves with some Catholic
social concepts.

But for this ham-actor on those stages it was the five priests
mentioned who made social doctrine a living Catholic reality. Pope
John XXIII twenty years later in *Mater Et Magistra* (No. 22)
would assert that "Catholic social doctrine is an integral part of
the Christian conception of life" but these men already held that
conviction from the writings of Leo XIII and Pius XI. They made
the social apostolate a central fact of their priesthood, although
teaching the encyclicals, organizing social action groups, were only
one element in their priestly ministry. Their approaches differed
with their personalities and as a result of the roles assigned to
them by the governing authorities of the Church.

John A. Ryan, then nearing the end of his days, was still the
premier theoretician of the American Catholic social movements.

His rooms in the old building of the National School of Social Service were poverty stricken by modern standards but adequate for the seminars and "bull sessions" which he delightfully chaired. His concepts and writings were the basis of lectures and courses for many years thereafter, not only in exalted universities but in humble parish halls too. Although he is often referred to now as "the Right Reverend New Dealer," because he advocated on behalf of the Church many programs—collective bargaining, unemployment compensation, social security, public housing, child labor reform—which later made Franklin D. Roosevelt an American legend, Ryan was detached from the daily political goings-on in Washington and could be rather objective about the New Deal itself, especially as it aged with himself.

Francis J. Haas, in many ways Ryan's most noted disciple, was a contrasting figure. He was practical minded and well-read more than theoretical, and politically oriented. Apart from his academic duties at the Catholic University of America, he developed into a first rate mediator for the U. S. Conciliation Service of the Department of Labor which took him deep into the councils of organized labor, especially the newer and struggling Congress of Industrial Organizations, and ultimately into the politics of government itself. He was personally close to the architects of the early New Deal legislation, with Robert F. Wagner, Sr., and Mary Norton who respectively championed the famous laws mandating collective bargaining and minimum wages. He was involved as a government official in the details of some of those "great" strikes in coal, automobiles, and steel which forged the present-day power of American labor. Even though he was a labor partisan, one learned from him the intricacies of a labor dispute and the amount of sweat which went into its resolution. He could be wryly humorous. Once, responding to a priest's objection to the closed-shop, Haas suggested that the last opponents of the closed shop should be priests who belong to the strongest closed-shop in the world. One did not come by the priesthood easily, but once in, the conditions of living were quite good and no one could be fired, even if the work performance was low. Though a quiet personality this Dean of Social Science influenced scores of priests who were seen annually at labor conventions. These proteges were delighted to see a man of his intellectual stance made a bishop of the Church, even if it was Grand Rapids and not Detroit.

Paul Hanly Furfey was destined to exercise a different kind of influence. The "fire on the earth" which he would see glow among men was "charity"—love of Christ and Christ's brothers. From the place where priest students usually sat, Furfey certainly came across as saintly, a description which today would embarrass him. Yet, while a denizen of Washington as much as Ryan, Haas or Parsons, he lived as though the important people in the city were not politicians but the poor. Decades before other social reformers, Furfey discovered the poor Blacks and the poor Chinese. His settlement house was a standing symbol of his own self-commitment and to those interested the personal prayer life of his associates made clear what the major priority of the Church was— union of man with God. While the rest of us were caucusing in comfortable hotel rooms about the nitty-gritty of wartime social problems, he was in the ghetto giving service, praying for non-praying brothers, teaching would-be-scholars how research in the streets was as important to the poor as that conducted in the still atmosphere of the Congressional Library.

Wilfred Parsons, former editor of *America* magazine, brought an entirely different dimension to the training of aspiring social scientists. He had two axes to grind which are worth mentioning: Catholic social doctrine was international in scope and its implementation depended on more than government. In Washington, D.C. of wartime vintage these were unusual perspectives. Ideology, even among Catholics, placed high value on national interests and the central role of government to problem solving. Social reformers, when they do not act as if making things right is their exclusive privilege, tend to share credit not with God to be sure, but with government, and especially with their own government. One night in Fr. Parson's small quarters in the Jesuit house, he led a discussion on Walter Lippmann's *U.S. War Aims* to highlight the socio-political problems created by a nationalistic approach to international difficulties. War was the issue then, not food distribution, nor poverty control. Those who argued for limited war aims debated those who supported ideological warfare. American public opinion to the contrary, the American government moved toward war in 1940 after the fall of France (not in 1939 after the fall of Poland) because Hitler's westward thrust threatened our command of the Atlantic Ocean, so vital to our commerce and our defense. The same nationalistic considerations—not ideology—subsequently prompted the same leadership to turn hegemony over Eastern Europe to the Russians because it was not vital to our security or well-being. Parsons, as a good Catholic political scientist, could not accept self-interest as the ultimate norm of moral value, but he was not unaware that as a social force self-interest can be a ferocious ally or enemy. Similarly he accepted the rightness of government economic activity without equating this with social reform and without identifying elected or appointed officials with the American state. In effect, he accepted any government new deal which improved the lot of citizens without being blind to the rigidities of government management.

John Patrick Monaghan shared two things in common with the others—a common priesthood and a social sense. In all other respects he was different. Irish born, a pastor of a parish, and, although friendly with the other four, was a local rather than a national influence. The Irish part of him made him a more spirited defender of the underdog wherever he was to be found. His long service as a parish priest, dealing in the practical order with many varieties of scalawags, gave him a sense of what worked and did not work.

Although a founder and later national chaplain of the Association of Catholic Trade Unionists, Monaghan stayed close to home among the social reformers of New York, where he exercised direct influence, part of which was due to his ability (God help us!) to use the King's English well. He could reduce an abstract concept to understandable words. Once speaking to an organizing meeting he said: "The job a man has supplies him with wages for food, clothing, and other necessities for himself and family. It is the most important thing in the world to him. A man's job is his life. Therefore, our economic world must accept the investment of a worker's mind and muscle as no less important than the money invested." It was work and trade unions (after the liturgy) which interested him most, even though he could put together $1,000 and a cow besides to help Dorothy Day out of a spot. His ACTU was for a time a vigorous layman's movement. "Doc" Monaghan, as he was affectionately called, exercised a fine priestly influence to be sure, but by his own admission learned as much from laborers, teachers and lawyers, as he taught them. He might counsel them about the foolishness of some contemplated action, but never interfered with their serious considered judgment, whether to throw a picket line against the offices of some prominent Catholic or around a Catholic cemetery.

Monaghan and his collaborators discovered early that, while "thieves" in places like Horn and Hardart cheated underpaid chefs and waiters, "thieves" were also to be found in the Longshoremen's and Teamsters' unions, men who pocketed graft and broke skulls, too. Helping workingmen see the importance of good wages through trade unionism became only one stage of ACTU's work. Labor schools could enlighten the depression poor about their rights under the law, but getting those rights from autocratic employers or criminals in the labor movement was quite another story.

The interesting fact is that after awhile ACTU was in difficulty not only with the money establishment but with the labor hierarchy too. Support by ACTU of a strike against employers was "progressive Catholicism." Opening up ACTU headquarters to disaffected unionists seeking to replace a corrupt labor leadership became "divisive Catholicism." The double standard was strange but understandable because the "party line" out of Washington rarely distinguished between good and bad strikes, between good and bad employers. Local Catholic activists close to particular scenes soon found that the encyclicals gave only the broadest guidelines about what to do with a fellow-travelling union leader giving aid and comfort to a Communist cause, or how to protect a decent employer from rival unions, and the city from a political strike which had nothing to do with working conditions.

Monaghan was firmly convinced that Catholic social effort—however much it might collaborate with other similar endeavors—could never be wedded inflexibly to entrenched positions or entrenched leadership. He was sensitive to the evaluations of the New York civic and Catholic communities and sought support at that level, but turned a deaf ear, if necessary, to policies or party lines promulgated far above where the action was. Contemporary poverty and minority groups face similar difficult choices. Local and national interests, especially in a large country like ours, very frequently exist in conflict. Even though people must fight their battles in local arenas there are not wanting national officials who evolve a "party line" which makes good reading on the front page but makes no sense to those wending their way through some local jungle. The party line is written in gray ink, when the issue is black and white, or vice versa. George Meany, for example, has belatedly discovered what his own state officials have known for a long time—the economic objectives of organized labor and the political aspirations of the Democratic Party are far from identical. Once upon a time the national office of Catholic bishops shuddered at local choosing up sides by groups like ACTU, but now bishops do the same thing. Blacks are beginning publicly to find flaws in some of their own organizations, a turn of events suggested but rejected ten years ago.

Five different priests—Ryan, Haas, Furfey, Parsons, Monaghan—came together in their common devotion to the Church whose priests they were. All of them, with the possible exception of Fr. Furfey, were conscious of how better the Church would be run by them, better than any bishop they knew. All could at times talk quite saltily about some of these same bishops. Many bishops had reason to disagree with anyone of them at any given time. Cardinal O'Connell took after a John Ryan about child labor and Cardinal Spellman had reason to be unhappy with John Monaghan about the Calvary strike. But in the end all of them received the endorsement of bishops and the Holy See.

Each of the five were in an independent way "community builders" with scores of disciples. But they never recognized any community of theirs as outside, certainly never against the Catholic community or the Church. They encouraged aggressive discussion and free-spirited activity from their own but never took part in, nor would they countenance, hostile behavior and disrespect toward the Church or its leadership. Some of those trained by them used to smile at overmoralizing theologians of great repute who knew what was wrong about stealing second base, but have no reason to be amused at prominent moralists of our day who find difficulty in moralizing at all, only to say "be of good conscience." A famous theologian recently called efforts to decide the liceity or illiceity of revolution to be moral imperialism, which supposedly is another form of despicable Catholic triumphalism. The sensible teachers, pastors, confessors of an earlier day followed the Church—its magisterium—not some crazy theologian. Now the same theologians are working hard to persuade the Catholic world that the bishops are really the crazy ones. The problems of those fighting for the new generation of the poor must learn where their roots really are, and their basic loyalties.

All this has relevance to the contemporary social question, because in the absence of the values and loyalties incarnated in the lives of those five pioneers, the Catholic Church has little to say of special significance to the world. Some things come out of a man's own gizzard and the uniqueness of his personal experience. But the best, if he wishes to talk for it, comes out of his own special tradition.

I write this book, for example, as a personal reaction to many things I have learned from my teachers. The book makes no pretense of doing justice to its title or the cause either of Church or poor. I did not intend in the beginning to inflict another book on a public wearied by current sadnesses; it grew out of a *colloquium* held more than a year ago with a handful of friends and a few co-workers at St. John's University in New York. We came together to discuss somewhat informally questions relating to the poor and our Church and the end result, beyond camaraderie and friendly interchanges, seems to be this book. I will be bold enough to quote some of the things they said, but because the context will be mine, I warn the reader to blame only me for excesses and defects. Some of these friends would stress other things and might even see the total picture differently. I do blame them, however, for being so knowledgeable and balanced in their views that I decided to write, however inadequately, on the subject matter specified by the title of this book.

Within the limits of this understanding I express, therefore, my appreciation to those friends who came once upon a time to St. John's University and stayed the right while; and among these I include:

Rev. Msgr. John Ahern, M.S.S.W., Director of Family Service, Catholic Charities, New York

The Honorable Hugh L. Carey (present Governor of New York)

Rev. Philip Carey, S.J., Xavier Institute of Industrial Relations, New York City

Miss Dorothy Day, Founder of The Catholic Worker Movement

Rev. Joseph I. Dirvin, C.M., Vice-President for University Relations and Secretary of the University, St. John's University, New York

Rev. Joseph Fitzpatrick, S.J., Chairman, Department of Sociology, Fordham University

Sister Grace, Apostolate of the Daughters of Charity, Mountain Districts of Virginia, bordering Appalachia

Most Rev. Timothy Harrington, Auxiliary Bishop, Diocese of Worcester, Massachusetts

Rev. Msgr. George G. Higgins, Director of Research, United States Catholic Conference, Washington, D. C.

Mr. Walter Hooke, Director of Personnel, United Parcel Service, New York City

Mrs. Dolores Huerta, President, United Farm Workers

Mr. Nicholas Kisburg, Legislative Director, Joint Council 16, International Brotherhood of Teamsters

Rev. Calvin Pressley, Director, Opportunities Industrialization Center, New York

It would be inappropriate also for me to conclude these remarks without a special word of gratitude to Fr. Joseph Cahill, C.M., and Fr. Joseph Dirvin, C.M., president and vice-president respectively of St. John's University, for their many excellent and sometimes unheralded contributions to the Church of our day and for their friendship and encouragement. Miss Carol Hand, my assistant, deserves an author's special blessing because she not only is a good researcher and editor, she typed every word of the manuscript herself.

GEORGE A. KELLY

CONTENTS

CHAPTER ONE

THE CHURCH AND THE POOR WHO ARE ALWAYS WITH US

"The Church must become without fear or favor the champion of the poor in our society."

MSGR. GEORGE G. HIGGINS

When the Carpenter of Nazareth told Judas, "The poor you have always with you but me you have not always,"[1] he created problems for his followers. One group of believers—the literalists —insist that the elimination of poverty and suffering is the responsibility of the total secular society, not the body of Christians as such. Triumphalists are assuming the double role of soul-saving and world-saving, alleging that the Church has always engaged in this two-fold enterprise. Scoffers and radical revolutionaries rest the authenticity of their particular social gospel on the fact that other-world viewing Christians do not know whether Christ meant poverty as a blessing or as a curse and, once successful themselves, tend with their religious leaders to be enemies of the poor they left behind. Writers on this general subject, therefore, tend instinctively to glorify the Church, damn her, or assign religious bodies in general to an irrelevant corner in all serious discussions of the question.

Ambivalence toward the poor, along with great charity, has always characterized the conduct of upper-class Catholics and some prelates. Contemporary writers point to the Church's vast holdings in real estate, its sizeable cash yearly income, to demonstrate how badly the first bishops have been served by the men who claim their place. Yet only blind commentators close their eyes to the lives and monies dedicated by religious bodies to uplifting the poor. A real argument gets under way when someone questions whether this effort really does any good. One non-Catholic scholar began his research because he was scandalized to learn that the Vatican owned 18 percent of a zinc mine in the Belgian Congo (Zaire). He wanted to know where this Catholic money was going and after several years of study and five hundred pages of text concluded:

> I think we should wish the Church well in its struggle for spiritual renewal and economic survival. Catholic or not, Christian or not, we gain by the work the Church does in education, in charity, in mercy. We also owe a debt to the Church as the curator of so much of our cultural heritage, and as the exemplar of the remarkable idea—remarkable at least in our time and our land—that money isn't everything.[2]

Some Catholic critics, on the other hand, are less understanding. To provide the poor with at least a cup of water, they would sweep away all the encrusted assets of the Church, along with the architectural masterpieces of history. Yet even critics, once they manage something of their own, learn that ideas, especially making ideas live, cost money. James Gollin shrewdly observed:

> Even a fluid, free-form church will need an economy. Every act of religion, ancient or modern, ceremonious or spontaneous, makes use of the things of this world; and regrettable though the fact may be, the things of this world cost money. Because a pilgrim church, like a Church Militant, marches on its stomach, someone will always have to worry about the state of the exchequer.[3]

The Social Gospel

The Church in many parts of the world still marches on its stomach and in the few affluent countries has marched with the poor beside. From the first appointment of deacons in Jerusalem (Ac 5) to the establishment four years ago in Washington of the *Bishops Committee on Farm Labor,* charged with the responsibility of supporting indigent migrant workers, even against the powerful International Brotherhood of Teamsters,[4] the Church has played an important poverty-role. What is now known as "the social doctrine of the Church" was not invented out of whole cloth or as a result of shrewd political judgment. The first Christians made social service a gospel must.[5] In fact, Jewish antecedents made their second contribution to the infant Church by handing on a tradition of alleviating suffering associated with penury. The patriarch Moses antedated Christians with a decree about Jewish obligation to the poor.

> The needy will never be lacking in the land, that is why I command you to open your hand to your poor and needy kinsmen in your country.[6]

New Testament leaders, following Christ's lead concerning the "world and the deceitfulness of riches"[7], required that perseverance be shown to poor men like Lazarus,[8] and warned followers about earthly goods, especially in relationship to the poor.[9] Paul, James, and John, by making a virtue of human concern for brothers in need of personal service[10] preached what is now called a "social gospel." The Fathers and Philosophers of the Church also made consistent efforts in the early centuries to apply these concepts to the events of successive centuries.[11]

The fact that so-called "Catholic Social Doctrine," as an organized body of thought, only appeared recently is evidence of what happened as a result of Capitalism and its offspring, Marxian Socialism. The poor were always there even in the thirteenth, "the greatest of centuries," but never so badly as in 1891 when Leo XIII took a look at "the condition of the working classes." Nineteenth century poverty uprooted children and wives from their families, destroyed husbands and fathers—while ruthless exploiters, who controlled both money and machinery and men absolutely amassed exorbitant wealth. In spite of these European cruelties, capitalism was offered as a dream, especially to young America. So entrancing were the alluring descriptions of fantasticized hopes for free enterprise, that even social minded Catholics were no more able than their non-Catholic contemporaries to commit themselves wholeheartedly to social reform. Hailing the virtues of American life, they could only with difficulty stress the need of reform.[12]

John Lancaster Spalding, progressive bishop of Peoria, rebuked the prophets of doom in this country and assured a Notre Dame graduating class late in the nineteenth century that the "organs of the social body" had never been so healthy.[13] The different perspectives of Leo XIII and American Catholics about the facts of social life were to haunt the Church for several generations.

In spite of American Catholic euphoria, Leo's worldwide view ultimately prevailed in the Church. *Rerum Novarum,* a description of the "miserable and wretched" conditions of the working-man, was the first major cohesive statement by a reigning pontiff on the right of the Church to intervene in the modern social order. Someone had to criticize the ruthlessness of capitalists, the inhumanity of employers, the unbridled greed of competitors. Leo decided that someone with power was the Church. But he did not get off easily. *Rerum Novarum* was "so utterly new to worldly ears" that forty years later Pius XI was forced to confess that the Church "was held suspect by some, even among Catholics, and to certain ones [Leo] gave offense."[14] By 1931 this newer Pope could assert with more secure authority that "the surest rules to solve the difficult problems of human relations called 'the social question'" came from a Pope.[15] *Divini Redemptoris* (1937), *Summi Pontificatus* (1939), *Mater et Magistra* (1961), *Pacem in Terris* (1963), *Populorum Progressio* (1968) followed. These encyclicals together comprise the magisterial teaching of the Church on social matters, whose authority is derived not only from revelation (and therefore only apply to Catholics) but reflect the necessary conditions under which human beings by the very demands of nature itself ought to live.[16]

The New Dreams of Men

All of that seems a long time ago. Yet merely two generations have passed. How much more complex is the economic world of

Paul VI? Equitable distribution of wealth may still be a "basic point in the program of Catholic social doctrine."[17] But there are new difficulties facing the Church. Yesterday's poverty was the perennial and irremediable lot of all but a favored few. Lower classes once were guaranteed a short biography simply by being born poor. Their shortened lives were dotted with chronic misery. The necessary virtues for survival were patience and long-suffering. Consolation came to the poor with the belief that their labors meant a better life for the children. Contemporary dreams are of an entirely different order. Even lower middle class Americans enjoy a standard of living beyond anything earlier centuries experienced, except in the castles of kings and rajahs. American poor savor the affluence all around them. And they want to taste its delicacy. Well-paid civil servants or trade unionists worry not about starving but about their ability to afford their own home. "Poor America" believe decent apartments without roaches or rats are their constitutional right. So well has Western capitalism advertised its wares, that those who have no money to buy what capitalists can sell are

> people who know that they no longer have to be hungry and poor, who want education and freedom, who want bicycles, refrigerators, movies and radios, who want to see the city, who want what science and technology made possible.[18]

This revolution in expectations—"we want prosperity now"— makes the otherwise patient poor angry, and more significantly changes his way of thinking about what is important in life. Their hunger for betterment affects family life style and religious beliefs. Once upon a time priests could say that "poor unfortunates kept their religious faith and feeling alive."[19] They can say that no longer. Not even the Protestant ethic, which equated poverty with moral delinquency, will be defended today. Public opinion, even among Catholics, may still associate prosperity with hard earned virtue, which is why middle-class citizens always vote against "give-aways," but blue-collar workers who have given consistent support to New and Fair Deal programs[20] are now the ones likely to accuse the newer poor of shiftlessness. What contemporary Catholics do not remember, or may be likely to forget, is that these charges were once directed against the "social degenerates" of another day—the Irish, those with high numbers in poor houses, jails, and orphan asylums.[21] The rebel priest, Edward McGlynn, got in trouble with his superiors because he dared to attribute the difficulties of the Church in the 1880's to the "foibles of the faithful."[22] Someone's morals may still be germane to particular poverty but in this era of social understanding poverty itself is the assigned villain. Dirty blocks, ugly and scarred tenements—"those tombstones of disease, unrest and smoldering violence"[23] so bitingly described by Irving Shulman in *The Amboy Dukes,* are miseries of life no longer acceptable. Neighborhoods with a majority of residents on welfare, with ancient schools staffed by disinterested teachers, with matriarchal households, now are inclined to fight, even if the people they fight are helpless too.

The Catholic Defense of the Poor Cause

Pope Paul VI, like his predecessors, places on the Church a double responsibility

to utter a unique message and to encourage the efforts of men who seek to take in hand and shape their own future.[24]

His concerns go beyond those of Leo XIII's workingmen. They embrace the "new poor," "people who suffer from bodily ills, who have trouble fitting themselves into society, the aged and those who are kept apart from society for one reason or another." In the nineteenth century, Popes did not pay special heed to "minority groups," "those who share a common household in the nation without equality before the law," nor to "migrants" who as "aliens" find it more difficult to claim their legitimate social rights. For Paul VI both minority groups and migrants are a world-wide problem.[25]

Bishops all over the world echo similar concerns. The 1971 Roman Synod, for example, made the poor cause the onus of Catholic bishops.

Listening to the cry of those who suffer violence and are oppressed by unjust systems and structures, and hearing too the appeal of a world that by its perversity contradicts the plan of its creator, we have taken account of the Church's vocation to be present in the midst of the world by proclaiming the Good News to the poor, freedom to the oppressed, and joy to the afflicted.[26]

While economic growth has made it possible "to feed the hungry at least with the crumbs falling from the table," this has proved to be a vain hope for many citizens of the world, one quarter of whose families regularly experience unemployment, "marginals" who are "ill-fed, inhumanly housed, illiterate, and deprived of political power as well as suitable means of acquiring responsibility and moral dignity."[27] The bishops ask: who will defend the dignity and fundamental rights of these people, if not the Church? Who will educate the major Western human families immersed with riches to these critical needs? Who is better qualified than the Church to lead this apostolate, especially since generation after generation of selfish materialists are the obvious products of modern educational systems?

The complacency of those who enjoy the benefits of unprecedented prosperity has become a major problem for warriors on poverty. Scientists presently maintain that there are few scientific or economic reasons for continuing poverty. Resistance to sharing the technological gains of modern society is mainly political and administrative. The United States cannot feed the world by itself but can *ad nutum* produce in greater abundance. Yet preferred national needs, public opinion about priorities, administrative obstacles to moving goods around, and "avaricious intermediaries, who prey on the poor" make solution-finding somewhat difficult, even for the best intentioned political bodies.[28]

Paul VI and Catholic bishops are quite realistic about all of this. They find these mental states and the moral habits of people to be great obstacles to reform. Noxious divisions between men of different races, cultures, religion, and politics are not likely to be bridged by technical arrangements or commanded by statute.

When statutes forbid the misuse of the poor minorities by the powerful, they are frequently manipulated to the advantage of the more astute and the powerful.

The Christian Ingredient

The proper solution will be discovered only in the general adoption of respect for human life. Christians must learn to feel a compunction to make their own the work of helping others in need. Prosperous Christians must voluntarily renounce some of their personal rights and advantages. These are hard sayings and preaching this gospel has never been easy. No one likes to be told: Physician, cure yourself. But the Church always has warned reformers that tinkering with institutions will never work to the advantage of the poor, if people themselves remained bad.[29] The false doctrine which makes law, technique, mechanism the chief human problem-solver is a deception. That policy will fail if its exclusive statements are: To distribute wealth, tax; to share power with the people, establish industrial councils. The good from such steps will largely be offset by effects which few people intended—the rich get richer, babies continue to be born in large numbers, a new group of "ins" prove more ruthless than displaced tyrants. The unregenerate heart and the evil mind of man have a long history of power within the best human structures. What the Church is saying, therefore, is that, for the affluent and for the poor too, the inner life is important to the long range cure of the inner city. Self-cure does not come easy to rich or poor. Franklin D. Roosevelt discovered this when he became a "traitor to his class," and Daniel P. Moynihan was castigated for suggesting that in addition to employment, improved family life was essential to Black prosperity.[30]

Majority groups are being challenged by the Church to take off their moral blinders to look more realistically at the seamy side of life and to sharpen their sense of justice and concern. They are challenged to liberate men from injustice because

unless the Christian message of love and justice shows its effectiveness through action in the cause of justice in the world, it will only with difficulty gain credibility with the men of our times.[31]

Minority groups, in the United States and elsewhere, are being encouraged to develop a new awareness of moral rights which are titles by which they "liberate themselves and become responsible for their own destiny." Popes and bishops claim as their very own this right and duty to call people to moral responsibility and to denounce moral shortcomings.

Declamations by ecclesiastics, however, amount to little more than pious pleading, unless the people in the pews make the cure of poverty their business. The gap that yawns between Catholic principles and Catholic practice does not escape the notice of bishops, who in a 1967 pastoral complained:

> Within recent years the Church has maintained the high level of its official teachings in encyclicals, in council, in synod, in papal addresses. She has borne dramatic witness to principle in *Mater et Magistra*, in *Pacem in Terris*, in the *Pastoral Constitution on the Modern World*, at the United Nations, and in *Populorum Progressio*. She has addressed herself to social justice, world peace, the political order, the underdeveloped nations. By all this, many were moved to put their hopes in her. If Catholic performance does not match Catholic promise, then truly we shall have failed.[32]

More than once, it has been said, the war on poverty will be won only when affluent peoples of the world are willing to pay the required price. If that judgment is at least partly so, then problem-solvers of poverty must look to the souls of men for the final results. Who shall make comfort-enjoying and humanistic sybarites accept poverty in spirit and justice toward the poor as virtues at all? How shall the eight beatitudes be inculcated? Governments obviously lack departments of spirituality. Hence, it falls to the Church to agitate the consciences of her own membership.[33]

The responsibility of the Church does not end there. Agreement on broad objectives and loosely defined moral norms contain too many escape hatches for the slothful. An unofficial historian of Lyndon Johnson's "war on poverty," when asked "Why didn't we eliminate poverty?" shrugged his shoulders and replied "We never really tried."[34] The Church has to make reluctant people try by specifying moral obligations with greater detail, by working to gain consensus among its own about those secondary steps, and then by praising or condemning as circumstances of success and failure multiply. Sanctions are what frequently give principles flesh and blood. The Church has great ability in this area when a central Catholic issue is involved. No great revolution in social attitudes or moral habits is likely unless the Church insists and dispenses its approvals and disapprovals accordingly.

There are at least five things the Church must expect from her people.

1. *Catholics Must Pray For The Poor*

Praying for the poor says something about the pray-er and his faith in the power of God to intervene in human history. Sophisticated humanists no longer believe that. Committed Christians are supposed to, and the poor, who have experienced divine interventions of which industrial whiz kids never dream, still have the old faith. Like the hard working Irishman whose hard labor made the farm much more productive than "when God had it all to himself," the Christian knows that prayer is no substitute for learning or for work. He also knows that men who rely on private Towers of Babel as solutions to human fears and human suffering end up babbling with one another. Prayer expresses faith in power greater than man's and is evidence of hope and patience. The blustery mother-figure in Sean O'Casey's *Juno and the Paycock* expressed possibly the playwright's doubts about the efficacy of prayer, when she asked: "What can God do against the stupidity of men?" But John A. Ryan more than three score years ago warned Catholic social workers against a secular approach to the poor. The primary function of the Catholic social ministry in his framework was

to bring the human soul into such relation to God, and to such harmony with God and his purposes, that it will be fit for a permanent union with God in the life to come.[35]

2. *Catholics Must Sympathize With the Poor*

Ever since the ascendant Protestant ethic placed high value on hard work and frugality, low value on contemplation, sociability, idle talk, too much sleep, and waste of time,[36] middle class people have had difficulty identifying with poor people. Lyndon Johnson began his war on poverty in the belief that "We shall overcome" whatever keeps people deprived, but his successor in the 1968 inaugural was closer to the standard American ethos when he demanded that Americans ask not what government can do for them, but what they can do for themselves. Harsh judgments about the poor are common to the American response, especially if Michael Harrington is correct in his assertion that recent poverty in this nation has become invisible to the typical citizen.[37] Once upon a time poor and rich lived with, beside, or near each other. Rich people saw poor people every day. The poor then were beneficiaries of "noblesse oblige," some hand-me-downs, and a bonus or two. But in more segregated urban areas of technopolis, the old time "deserving poor," especially those with a different skin color or language, easily become "undeserving." Now that there are no redeeming social relationships between classes, there is no guarantee of interest, let alone sympathy. Even the latest benefactor of the poor—government—frequently is judged to do more harm than good.[38] As a result, programs designed to alleviate poverty, end up alienating the very people whose public support is necessary to the elimination of poverty.[39]

This may only prove that men cannot be expected to be reasonable about situations in which they have no vital stake. Myth and self-interest prevail over facts and sanity. All data to the contrary, the belief that the overwhelming majority of those below the classic poverty line are drunks, addicts, loafers, scoundrels remains solidly held. Comparatively few look out of their own way station to see an abandoned child and mother, the aged mother or father, the blind, the lame, the halt, the mentally unbalanced, the retarded, those who cannot find work because there is no work, those who do not work because no one will hire their kind. Catholics, recently up from poverty, ought to be natural sympathizers but are not. John Cort, who spent the better part of thirty years with movements of social reform, once asked a friend why the labor movement, which in many ways is so Catholic, had become so conservative? His reply was direct: "Well, it's the first time that we've had anything to conserve."[40] That is a plain truth which explains the hard heart, yet leaves it untouched.

How then to touch that hard heart? One industrialist decided that the way to do this was to put management officers in direct contact with the poor. He established an *Urban Internship Program* for up-and-coming executives, which required their presence for as long as three months in settlement houses, recreation centers, interracial activities, training programs for the ghetto. The end result of the internship was that these managers—whose later success depended on how they dealt with a variety of citizen types—were forced to confront their own assumptions about the poor, many of whom became their workers and customers, to confront their own ignorance, to develop empathy for those locked into oppressive living conditions.

Some of the written reactions to the internship illustrate the value of personal involvement as a means of moving hearts. One personnel manager from New Mexico described his lesson as follows:

> A rap session with a welfare recipient proved to be a real shocking experience. The problems this woman and her family had getting on welfare and then staying on the program were disgusting to say the least. The first year they were on the program, the Welfare Department provided them a $500-a-month motel room. After the first year they were moved to a very poor, temporary housing where they have since been living.
>
> After hearing about the problems this family had in collecting their welfare checks twice a month, one can understand why many steal rather than try to collect welfare. The woman commented that she would have to start stealing in order to

feed her three children. Also, after hearing about the problems encountered by two interns who carried a seventy-two year old lady to the Medicaid office, one begins to realize the problems that exist within our government agencies.[41]

A Washington State man explained the discovery he made on the East Coast.

It soon became apparent that the people living on the Lower East Side, young and old alike, are no different than you or I. They have the same desires as we, the same needs, but they do not have the same opportunity. They are left alone in their own world, forgotten by the only people who could change the conditions.[42]

A manager from Southern Illinois found out what it was like to be a welfare recipient.

I would like every middle class American to spend some time talking to the people that must survive under the conditions of welfare. I feel fortunate to have spent some time with a lady who was eighty-three years old and on welfare. Because she had an income of $1.53 a month more than the amount you are allowed to make or receive, the Welfare Office was in the process of taking away her medical benefits under Medicare. The people at Henry Street had gotten her a hearing before the Welfare Board. It was my assignment to take her and see that she was given a fair hearing and see that all the facts were brought out.

I waited in line while she sat outside the Welfare Office for four and a half hours. Once inside I was given a number. After another two and a half hours I was finally allowed to talk to the hearing officer. He listened to the facts and said there wasn't anything he could do; another hearing date would have to be set. I said that it was not possible because of the medicine needed by this lady. After discussing the matter for another half hour with this gentleman, I was sent next door to another building and after talking only five minutes, the lady's medical benefits were restored.

It is hard to understand how people on welfare have the patience to deal with the red tape and the struggle they must go through to barely survive. You have to sit at a Welfare Office to believe that people really are being given such inhuman treatment. The lack of concern and inefficiency of the Welfare Department is deplorable.[43]

3. Catholics Must Themselves Become Personalists

In spite of shortcomings and a late arrival on the American scene, Catholics have been more social reform-minded than the general American population. Robert Cross, who was critical of nineteenth century Catholic social reform, has very little complaint in this regard about twentieth century Catholics.[44] He learned what the sociologist Gerhard Lenski also discovered, that on public issues of a social nature Catholics tend to be welfare statist.[45] Andrew Greeley and Peter Rossi believe that common descriptions of Catholics as social reactionaries are lying-stereotypes. Education, particularly in a succession of Catholic schools, has made Catholics somewhat socially progressive.[46] The public figures largely responsible for early social welfare programs often have been Catholic—Robert Wagner, Philip Murray, Mary Norton. New issues have emerged, apparently more important than the size of the weekly pay check, to turn Catholics away from welfare statism. But not even this partial swing to the right justifies the abuse sometimes heaped upon Catholics for their alleged failure to support the Blacks and Hispanics who took their place in the urban jungle. Somewhat belligerently Daniel Moynihan attributes the loss of Catholic municipal power to this very failure.[47]

The fact is that Catholics need a better press agent or scholars interested in some friendly facts. Catholics only began to make it—after World War II—about the time Blacks and Hispanics began to move North, East, and West. The concern of Catholics was keeping it made and having babies. "Taking care of our own" became a priority, especially for those on the fringes of the middle-class. Moving out of tenements was a sign of moving up the American ladder and if Irish and Italian Catholics did not look back on those taking their places in the old ghetto, it was because they were struggling too. Some climbers were hostile to Blacks and Puerto Ricans, but most were merely concerned with their own improvement. Catholic leadership, however, did take notice of the new poor. Bishops like Joseph Ritter in St. Louis, Robert Lucey in San Antonio, Joseph Rummell in New Orleans, Patrick O'Boyle in Washington, Vincent Waters in Raleigh were ahead of most public officials on matters such as integration of schools and housing. *Catholic Interracial Councils* constantly reminded church bodies, almost totally white, that the apostolate to poor Blacks was a Catholic Commitment. Whenever Catholics were inclined to be smug, laymen like Matthew Ahmann, one-time executive director of the *National Catholic Conference for Interracial Justice,* pounded home unmercifully the complaint:

> Any observation on the role of the Church in the 'urban racial crisis' must recognize the guilt the Church shares for the way racial minorities have been exploited in our society.[48]

Indeed the very ferocity of the attacks of Catholics on other Catholics was itself evidence of a lively growth of personalism within the Church. Lily-white churches were looked upon as symbols of the lack of contact between whites, browns, blacks. Personal piety, daily Masses, novenas, missions were dismissed as preoccupations with personal salvation in the great beyond to the exclusion of concern for the hell lived by the poor only a mile away. Silent majorityship and respectability were labeled an affront to the real Jesus. How could the Man of Jerusalem who "stirred up" his people against the multiple mistreatment of the poor in his day be represented by self-satisfied suburbanites? Some critics did not think it possible for these types to be renewed, let alone saved. In return, the criticized Catholics quite rightly looked over their shoulder to ask: "Are they speaking of us?" They were painfully aware that the favors done personally for the poor or money privately contributed to their uplift, seemed lately to count for nothing. It was as if Catholic social commentators, like the Marxists, were blaming such charity for the continued failure of radical social reform.[49] Yet local Catholics were more sensible than high-level experts. People still go hungry, face eviction from their homes, children need heat, clothes, schooling, and in large metropolitan areas aged poor die in increasing numbers without anyone to bury them. Public agencies, for all their value, are never quite present at such moments. Or, as interested pastoral ministers can testify, the public service performed is often rendered callously. The soothing hand of a nun, the supporting voice or presence of the St. Vincent de Paul Man, the Lady of Charity, and/or Big Catholic Brother or Sister, the little noticed or hardly ever counted gift of food, clothes, furniture or money are always just what the doctor ordered for the moment.[49]

One sociologist, who has been highly critical of the Church's performance in several areas, readily acknowledges that

> indictment of the Churches may appear somewhat exaggerated to readers who recall the extensive efforts of the Churches to develop social programs.[50]

Part of the reason for the slight is that in the last forty years Catholic historians and sociologists have been more entranced with the virtues of government programs, and less with the total day-to-day workings of the Church.

Several years ago Timothy Costello, president of Adelphi University, when asked as deputy mayor of New York whether the Church perchance was behind the times, remarked: "The Church may be fifty years behind the times, but let me tell you, government is fifty years behind the Church. Show me the government which has 'Little City Halls,' thousands of committed volunteers devoting full time to people, in every neighborhood of the country."[51] He was referring of course to Catholic parishes and Catholic institutions. Government bureaucracies today are making serious efforts at the same kind of decentralization—getting out of Washington and back to the states, away from City Hall down to the community. The Catholic Church daily wakes up with 30,000 organized groups in every local neighborhood of the nation.[52] St. Vincent de Paul men alone gave 4,876,000 volunteer service hours to the poor across the country.[53] Disgruntled critics look upon these social structures as comfort stations for the saved, defenders of the cultural status quo, and pious assemblies of political nobodies.[54] Yet, even if less than optimum performance is attributed to the 200,000 priests and religious who staff these bodies, services are being provided for people in the low and low middle class category, more comprehensive than that provided by any other private institution. That in itself is quite unique and not sufficiently credited.

4. *Catholics Must Continue Their Generosity to Poor Causes*

Consider the amount of money contributed by Catholic Americans to the poor of all descriptions in all corners of the globe. After paying their own rent, grocery bills and their taxes, after keeping their parishes and their increasingly burdensome parochial schools going, Catholics last year gave in the neighborhood of $200,000,000 to causes and movements aiding the poor somewhere in the world. This is a lot of money from a working people whose millionaires are few. Only half of the 50,000,000 Catholics regularly attend Mass,[55] and, as any working pastor can guarantee, about forty percent of the Mass-attenders carry the burden of every Catholic cause. In actual fact, only ten million Catholics support the Church's national and international relief efforts. Were the federal government comparably successful in attracting such voluntary donations, enough cash would be available to raise the minimum assistance of the poor in low income states to levels of respectable decency.[56]

Every American diocese has a Catholic Charities' organization established to administer goods and services to the poor—neglected and dependent children, the aged, the sick, the delinquent. Larger archdioceses work on annual budgets financed by voluntary contributions amounting to $5,000,000 each. The 200 diocesan organizations together collect over $50,000,000 a year. This becomes "seed money," attracting ten times that amount in government grants to Catholic institutions and programs. These totals take no account of vast millions collected by religious orders for their own special apostolates, most of which in one shape or another are directed to the poor. Neighborhood Ozanam groups alone made $13,000,000 available to families in 1973.[57] More than half of all the monies disbursed through the world-wide Society of the Propagation of the Faith—$20,000,000—comes from the American people.[58] The beneficiaries are the people of Ambatu (Equador), Papua (New Guinea), Masoro (South Africa) and places no one on the outside knows exist but the Church.

An equally important tribute to American Catholic ingenuity is the goods and services provided by Catholic Relief Services. In 1974 the total amount of goods and services provided by the American bishops to the poor of Bangladesh, Jerusalem, Yemen, Laos, Macao, Upper Volta, Chad, Honduras, were valued at $154,089,-262. Since its founding in 1943 CRS has disbursed $2.46 billion of relief to the world's poor. Edward Kinney, executive director, made this claim about the work of his agency.

> No other agency in the history of American voluntary aid has distributed as much supplies to as many of the war-stricken, the refugees and displaced persons, the victims of disaster and emergencies, and to the indigenous poor throughout the developing world.[59]

5. Catholics Must Engage in Social Action

If a review of the facts or testimony of the poor themselves properly credit the scope of Catholic Charity, well-nigh universal among those who write on the subject is disdain for Catholic social action programs. This is particularly true of those who never personally led a social crusade of their own. The word "charity" has become a dirty word in America, even among Catholics who should better remember it as a New Testament word for love. Overturning institutions has become the social imperative more than charism, the other gospel word for love. Pedestrian activity such as feeding the hungry, clothing the naked, teaching a child to read and write receive short shrift. Marxian socialism apparently has acquired a late day in the Catholic sun. Bread alone matters, particularly that bread which is wrung from the hands of some exploiter, by violence if necessary. The new breed of reformer, while usually mouthing phrases of non-violence, frequently endorse class conflict under the name of "affirmative action."

Extremists are never satisfied with peaceful and moderate progress, nor do they like to acknowledge that the Catholic Church has not been a failure, even in the area of social action. From the time that the American Church ceased being an immigrant enclave, (World War I is as good a dividing date as any) bishops well in advance of the New Deal led the nation in proposing minimum wages, protection of the right to organize, insurance against the hazards of unemployment, accident and old age, the construction of public housing and better methods of conciliating labor strife. Bishops, whose basic business is turning men to God, not higher wages, required some prodding, not only from Rome, but from some of their own priests. John A. Ryan, William Kerby, Peter Dietz were early on the scene. Later all over the country priests, quite well-known in their own chancery offices, became aggressive agitators for trade unionism and social legislation. The list of such priests is quite impressive: Thomas Shortell (Boston), William Kelly, William Smith and Joseph Hammond (Brooklyn), John Boland (Buffalo), Reynold Hillenbrand, Daniel Cantwell, George G. Higgins (Chicago), Francis Gilligan and Francis Flanagan (Cincinnati), Francis Carney (Cleveland), Virgel Michel (Collegeville), Raymond Clancy (Detroit), Joseph Donnelly (Hartford), Louis J. Twomey and Vincent O'Connell (New Orleans), John Monaghan, Thomas Darby, John Byrne (New York), Denis Comey (Philadelphia), Charles Owen Rice (Pittsburgh), John Friedel, Leo Brown, Richard McKeon (St. Louis), Bernard Cronin (San Francisco), Francis J. Haas, Raymond A. McGowan and John F. Cronin (Washington, D. C.). These labor priests were only part of a social apostolate which included John La Farge, George Hunton, Peter Maurin, George Donahue, John Cort, Dorothy Day, Dorothy Dohen working frequently only in the world of inter-race and poverty. Laymen like Paul Weber (Detroit) and

Roger Larkin (New York), as executives of the ACTU and editors of the *Wage Earner* and *Labor Leader* respectively, packed a good deal of local social action wallop, even if they were rarely featured in the national magazines or are now well-remembered. The catalogue of pioneers remains incomplete without the names of priests such as Robert Keegan and Bryan J. McEntegart, who are chiefly responsible for relating the voluntary effort of Catholic social agencies to the burgeoning welfare bureaucracy of the federal government. They secured quasi-public status for private religious effort in social service which perdures to this day.

The *Catholic League for Social Justice,* the *Catholic Worker,* the *Catholic Interracial Council,* the *Association of Catholic Trade Unionists,* the *Christian Family Movement* all functioned in some dioceses more than others, sometimes with an enthusiastic *imprimatur,* but always with a *nihil obstat.* Stereotype statements about these sometimes frenetic activities suggesting that "some bishops were lukewarm in their support and many of the laity were recalcitrant"[60] are intended to imply that positive contributions to social reconstruction were freakish deeds of freakish men. During depression years priests all over the country, later on Brothers and Sisters too, were quite involved in poverty causes. Sometimes they helped the C.I.O. gain respectability. Later they made the march on Selma respectable. Those who loudly insist bishops are not the Church are the very ones who deny the Catholic community's involvement, unless the bishop is not on the picket line too. Complainers never ask why bishops should be choosy about their picket lines. Determining in advance which picket line really promotes justice is sometimes a simple decision, sometimes an exercise in legerdemain. John Cogley, summing up his experience in Chicago and New York, is convinced that

> many Catholics, including some important bishops and other highly placed Churchmen, took a somewhat dim view of any concrete involvement.[61]

and also is quite certain that priests who were involved

> did not always enjoy the confidence of their superiors and

were looked upon as clerical rabble-rousers by a significant number of the laity.[62]

To combat this kind of judgment is never easy. Andrew Greeley, another Chicagoan, in one of his syndicated columns during the summer of 1973, bluntly criticized Cogley as "a journalist who has specialized for decades in interpreting American Catholicism to the liberal and intellectual elites in such a way as to do very little to disturb their prejudices."

Perhaps this is just about where the Church will always be with critics—facing prejudices which criticize failure and inadequate performance by churchmen, but rarely and never equally crediting its ministers with good works or good intentions. Catholics, including bishops, are judged poor leaders in any field including social action. But many too are unheralded for their sanity in not buying any pig-in-a-poke.

The real prize of the Church, rarely acknowledged, is the freedom of sub-alterns at all levels to engage in all kinds of social activity without interference. No Catholic is obligated to accept a *German Catholic Central Verein* or a *Catholic Temperance Union* or a *Catholic Worker* or a *National Federation of Priests Council* as the approved method of dealing with a social problem. Those who seek the prior endorsement of higher authority seem to suggest endorsement, not the work itself, is the primary value. Those involved in public service of these kinds are grateful for whatever encouragement or promotion or blessing enlarges the significance of what they do. But official approval always comes late even to Francis of Assisi and Elizabeth Seton. Saints, better than most, can explain the care which must be exercised in placing the whole weight of the Church behind someone's specialized apostolate. Ecclesiastics, once they decide the good of the faith is involved, frequently on advice act against their own better judgment or their own personal feelings. But they are entitled to some convincing about where the best interests of the Church lie.

One school of Catholic thought believes that, in spite of social pioneers, the Church has "failed to establish a strong tradition of reform interest."[63] To offset the social reforming magnificence of

John A. Ryan, Robert Lucey or Joseph Rummell, the minor and reactionary efforts of Edward Keller or Clarence Manion, neither of whom will live in history, are given historical importance to which they have no claim. Churchmen such as Francis J. Spellman and his one-time Vicar General, J. Francis A. McIntyre, are rarely evaluated on the things they did to champion social justice. Each on occasion could be highly critical of the Social Action Department of their own *National Catholic Welfare Conference,* and personally opposed the involvement of Catholics in conflicts like the Wall Street Strike in 1948. The other part of the same record is that lay Catholics and priests were involved on a day to day basis in both these situations, incurring at the worst only the momentary displeasure of one bishop. Spellman will never live down the ignominy of allowing himself to become personally involved in a labor dispute between Catholic gravediggers and the priest-director of his cemeteries. Introducing seminarians as strike-breakers was merely adding insult to injury. Officials with the ear of the bishop can always alarm him, as happened in this case, about communist control of a union which in the Calvary situation was not a fact. Interestingly, the same conservative McIntyre, later Archbishop of Los Angeles, hearing of that strike shook his head and commented: "Had I been still in New York that strike would not have occurred." Even though the Calvary strike was a disastrous even for the Church, Spellman's allies through the years of his administration continued to be labor leaders up to and including George Meany. Even the final agreement with gravediggers became a model for other cemeteries. Throughout the quarter of a century following, Catholic cemeteries in New York have been relatively strike-free, as much a testimony to Spellman as it is to anyone.

Spellman by personality was not given to public crusades. Yet on a given issue he was capable of taking a strong stand sometimes against strong voices. His decisive support of religious freedom and John Courtney Murray at Vatican II made him a momentary hero to those ordinarily not partial to his ecclesiastical style. Whenever the real issues were public housing for the poor or mean treatment of non-Catholic Black diocesans, he could be as strongly vocal as when he spoke on patriotism and obscenity. Little noticed at the time of the march on Washington in 1963 was Martin Luther King's praise of New York's support. Spellman's life membership in the National Association for the Advancement of Colored People was less known. Prior to that march Spellman issued a devastating critique of the race problem which was made must-reading in everyone of his four hundred churches. Forgotten now are some of his strong words:

> There is simply no reason—there never was and there never can be—why the color of a man's skin should limit his opportunities in a society that boasts of freedom.

> Americans who risked their lives for America—for you and for me—are denied the right to vote, the right to receive an adequate education, the right to live where they desire and their means enable them to live and to receive the normal courtesies befitting their dignity as human beings. They are denied these rights for only one reason—the color of their skin. How lamentable that some Americans who would die together today, will not eat together, will not travel together, will not live together. This is an outrage which America cannot tolerate. Doors cannot continue to close in the face of Negroes as they search for jobs, as they strive for membership in some unions, as they seek the change for specialized job training.[64]

Less than two years later he came back to the priests and the people with a more urgent call for their personal involvement in the question of racial harmony. On March 14, 1965 he wrote:

> The frightening disturbances in Selma, Alabama culminating in the martyrdom of the Reverend James Reeb, are a tragedy for America and must awaken the consciences of all who are fair-minded and against the evil of violating the basic rights of men. Racial and civil injustice are a cancer attacking the very life of our nation and society. Their eradication is the urgent concern of all Americans and we cannot disassociate ourselves from this great challenge.[65]

The "official" Church will in the eyes of men in the field always seem to have an uneven record of civic involvement. Even the generous approach to human problems by a Bernard J. Sheil of Chicago or a Richard J. Cushing of Boston will have critics who point to their bad administrative record or the size of their final indebtedness which some successor liquidated.

What is also frequently forgotten about the Catholic social action apostolate is that not everyone has an aptitude for this work. A strong tradition within the American Church for social reform does not mean, as John XXIII in *Mater et Magistra* made clear, that this apostolate is for everyone.[66] Thirty years before him Pius XI declared:

> It will be essential to begin, not with great numbers, but with small, well-trained teams who will act as a sort of evangelical leaven to transform the whole mass.[67]

What perhaps is a fairer question for judgment is whether the Church has or can develop actively involved leaders. John L. Thomas is inclined to think not. He argues that the churches, all of them, have

> not been able to produce a creative elite capable of dealing with the unending task of developing, modifying and adjusting means that would adequately assure the realization of desired goals.[68]

Contrariwise, there is another more hopeful interpretation of the realities of Catholic life. Catholics may not seem to have leaders of large crusades, but in every city of the country they do have a lot of "little" Martin Luther Kings. Hardly a social program of any kind gets off the ground, or functions, without the significant leadership of one Catholic or another. While Sargent Shriver or Hugh Carey in government, Theodore Hesburgh or Ivan Illich in racial and ethnic affairs, Andre Hellegers in health or William B. O'Brien in drug therapy do not represent all that is saintly in the Church, they do symbolize the larger body of Catholics hard at work locally on evils associated with the status quo. Some of these will not likely become footnotes of history for the reason that they are not infamous.

Catholic leaders sometimes are unacceptable to the secular powers because they say the wrong thing or want the wrong thing undone. Charles J. Bonaparte, Secretary of the Navy under Theodore Roosevelt, once deplored the price often exacted from the Church by civil government. He correctly admonished his fellow religionists:

> Caesar does not work for nothing: he must be paid for his protection; if he makes heresy treason, he asks that she make treason heresy, and this is little less than a ruinous price for a less than doubtful service.[69]

Everytime a Catholic leader or Catholic organization is locked into someone else's machinery, the same *quid pro quo* is expected. Pope Paul from on high may safely criticize social actionists for their shortcomings, the wrongs they commit and the "conditions (they impose) which are too burdensome for the overall economy of society."[70] But few Catholics are likely to be appointed to powerful commissions or boards after they indicate hostility to the man in the White House, or suggest that some corporate policy is sinful, or that labor and community leaders have built up private bank accounts on poor people's money. The outspoken Catholic critic of the secular establishment, of left, right, or no ideology, likely finds himself written off as a "pinko," a "fascist," a "racist."

The bloodline of democracy is trading over or under the table. The reality of politics is the sell-out of one issue to gain some other advantage. Catholics have been known to play this game well, although some lose their integrity or their Catholicity in the process. To be accepted in the right social circles, Catholics must sound like Democrats, Republicans, Business Executives, Labor Leaders, Social Activists, and not like men pushing the Kingdom of God on earth. To stay in these "clubs" they have to accept the conditions of admission and adopt their values. Peter Berger states the fact candidly: "Birds of a feather flock together not as a luxury but out of necessity."[71]

It will never be easy, therefore, for the committed Catholic with conscientious moral principles to "pass over" into the club and yet retain—as men like Charles De Gaulle did—their Catholic identity and piety. In the last century some who tried became Protestant. Some new integrationists became either racists or violent witnesses to a relatively colorblind and peaceful gospel. One special danger is canonization by the press. Catholics, even the scholars who enjoy the favor of reporters, frequently are those who prefer public to Catholic education, who endorse contraception, divorce, abortion, or homosexuality. The dominant secular establishment wants these values for the nation and their Catholic promoters are easily credited as representing the progressive forces in the Church. Involved Catholics who privately battle pretentious lawmakers, draw attention to agents of the poor living off the poor's crying needs, object to distributing contraceptives to teen-agers or the enrichment of abortionists, will likely find themselves excluded from the "right seminars and cocktail parties." Civil religionists are affronted by the orthodox religious. Their ethos clashes with traditional doctrine on the very idea of a personal God and a divine way of doing things. In Max Weber's highly rationalized society, which makes efficiency the eternal principle of life, even Papal encyclicals smack of obscurantism.

So, those Catholics who are anxious to swim with the American mainstream, a desirable goal in itself, especially the aspiring professionals, must face up to the testing whenever an Uncle Tom role is proffered. They may end up talking for the voice of America but not from the deck of Peter's Barque. This is not a temptation for most Catholics because they are too busy just surviving. The Gilbert Chestertons, Hilary Bellocs, and Frank Sheeds of this day will always act like secure and free Catholic witnesses because they enjoy remarkable talent and are good prayers. Would-be Don Luigi Sturzos will have a more difficult time because choosing Caesar over God is very attractive and the line between accommodation and betrayal is so easily blurred. The days of Alfred E. Smith are not exactly gone. To gain public stature of major significance the Catholic candidate must put some distance between the Church and himself, perhaps even imply that Liberal Protestant theology is now good Catholic orthodoxy.

These comments are not pleasant to make but are points of view which must be confronted honestly by those who in the Church's name would help Protestant Blacks and Catholic Hispanics, each lacking their own priests to explain what Catholic social action is or ought to be, and what it may not be.

In-house fighting among the Irish, Italians, and Germans represented a type of family squabbling which contributed to ultimate Catholic unity. The bitter sentiments alleged to exist in the newer ghettos against all white establishments, including Churches, may not lead to such a happy conclusion, if the dominant voices continue to be those whose power depends on inflammation and disruption.

Social action today takes place in groups intended to mobilize the poor to act on their own behalf. The OEO programs represented a departure from earlier philanthropic or social service models, because they shifted muscle power to agencies managed by the poor themselves. *The Citizens' Crusade Against Poverty* stated in 1964 its blunt objective.

> The fight against poverty must not become merely a well-intentioned social welfare program in which the 'haves' do favors for the 'have-nots.' The poor must be enabled to share in the sense of dignity and belonging that only their personal and active participation in the struggle can provide.[72]

Coordinating groups patterned after *Citizens' Crusade* are still determined to exact their rightful pound of flesh from the federal government. They even resented the fact that original funding came from labor unions, civil rights groups, and churches since

> labor unions have not been particularly concerned with opening up opportunities or mobilizing power for change in the status of minority poor. The churches and the civil rights groups have consistently verbalized concern for the poor but so far have not found the formula for playing an effective role in existing programs, and themselves have not, for many and

unclear reasons, been able to mount a national or direct local program for action on behalf of the poor.[73]

Educators, like Kenneth Clark, denied that these traditional groups benefit the poor because "the predicament of the poor has become steadily more desperate."[74] Like it or not, community action groups take aim at local merchants, slumlords, municipal officials up to and including the mayor. The complaints made about their tactics or the quality of their leadership are hardly different than criticism of labor unions from an earlier generation. Rent strikes, marches on city halls, even legal suits financed with federal money against the government itself continue to be essential ingredients of this crusade. Catholics are involved as promoters, protectors, and critics of these approaches, which have become regular activities for increasing numbers of priests, religious, and laity.

But this does raise a question about the particular competence of religionists *qua* religionists. The Church has never claimed any technical competence for solving the problems of economics, sociology, politics, or medicine. It is, says the Church, politicians drawing on experts who really count. There are those who pretend the situation was otherwise, but Paul VI takes the realistic view in saying:

> In the social and economic realm, whether on the national or international level, the ultimate decision rests with political authority.[75]

This is no cop-out. A sensible delineation of roles, a clear line of demarcation between the sacred and the secular, between providing the bread of eternal life and this life's wonder bread, are essential. The Church has her own special weapons against injustice, but they do not include balancing international payments, inflating or controlling prices, providing guaranteed incomes or medical care. These works of civil society are the very reason governments were created among men. Trade associations, labor unions, political clubs, cultural organizations also belong to the secular sphere.

Catholics should join them and in secular deliberations hopefully will conduct themselves as Catholics. But not even the most saintly apostle has any mission from the Church to exercise any special authority within these organizations, even if they were one hundred percent Catholics. As arms of the state they play the game according to civil rules.[76]

This does not mean that the Church stands completely aloof from temporal matters. The "noxious tendency," a favorite expression of Pius XII, must be resisted which would confine the Church to the sanctuary or to purely religious matters. The human struggle is a Church struggle, too. The Church wants citizens to organize in their own interests. Catholic schools and associations are charged with the responsibility of pricking the social conscience of their students. The state has a right to receive good citizens and upright officers from the Church. The institutional Church necessarily collaborates with civic groups whenever people are in misery. Her preachments of the social gospel help; so do her suggestions for particular situations. Passing judgment on the conduct of political leaders or social institutions is not without benefit to the community, so that specific social policies, whether a prohibition of liquor sales, a right to work law, a segregation bill, or a labor management conflict are amended or vitiated.[77]

Interventions by the Church occur to greater or lesser extent as the circumstances warrant. They are not always appreciated by those holding power. Franklin Roosevelt resented Catholic criticism in the latter half of his presidency, no less than Republicans resented the preachments of Catholic social doctrine. Old line A.F.L. leaders resented the seeming partialities shown to the C.I.O. newcomers. The Church rarely intervenes directly in the political process except when her own institutional needs are threatened. The freedom to teach religion in Poland or the effective right to run parochial schools in the United States are cases in point.

However, the social doctrine of the Church or anyone else would never be realized in the practical order, if preaching, forming consciences, or nagging were all there was to the Catholic thing. Organized groups within society and government itself have the competence and the authority to determine what alternatives are correct for this time, are likely to obtain popular approval, and have a reasonable chance of success. These decisions call for highly intricate economic and political knowledge plus a great deal of good fortune. This is why highly motivated and assuredly professed Catholics are on their own when practical decision-making is required.

The very complexity of the political process explains why the Church is hostile to the involvement of priests in the process. Political priests have to be somewhat saintly but they also have to appear above the common, often ugly fray. The Church does not rule out priestly politicians in trade associations, labor unions, government bodies for as Pius XII once said:

> The priest has as good an eye as the layman to discern the sign of the times and his ear is not less sensitive to the human heart.[78]

But by and large the partisan involvement of priests in controversies which set faithful against faithful has only exacerbated contention. Sometimes the Church whose leadership must always be prepared to reconcile factions in parishes or communities, has been shamed by warring priests. The end result is frequently bad politics and bad priests.

Even if all else falls short of the best expectations of the Church, even granting less than success to energetic and skillful efforts of her members, there is still one on-going role that only the Church can play. By preaching to make men aware of a better kingdom to come, invitations which are extended to those who have completed a successful pilgrim voyage. And a sign of a good pilgrimage is effective assistance to those most neglected by the world.

NOTES FOR CHAPTER ONE

1 John 2:8.

2 James Gollin, *Worldly Goods,* (New York: Random House, 1971), p. 497.

3 *Ibid.,* 33.

4 The Teamsters' Union through their Western Conference was determined to destroy the infant United Farm Workers which four years earlier had succeeded in organizing fruit and vegetable pickers as no one before had done. See Winthrop Griffith, "Is Chavez Beaten?" *New York Times Magazine,* September 15, 1974, pp. 18 ff.

5 Igino Giordani, translated by Alba I. Zizzamia, *The Social Message of Jesus,* (Paterson, New Jersey: St. Anthony Guild Press, 1943); *The Social Message of the Early Church Fathers,* (Paterson, New Jersey: St. Anthony's Guild Press, 1944).

6 Dt 15:2.

7 Mt 13:22.

8 Lk 16:1-31.

9 Mk 25:31-46.

10 Gal 3:28; Col 3:2; 1 Cor 12:13; 1 Jn 2:15 ff.

11 Paul Hanly Furfey, *A History of Social Thought,* (New York: The Macmillan Co., 1949), pp. 156-183.

12 Robert D. Cross, *The Emergence of Liberal Catholicism in America,* (Cambridge, Massachusetts: Harvard University Press, 1967), p. 108.

13 *Ibid.*

14 Pius XI, *On Reconstructing the Social Order,* (Washington: National Catholic Welfare Conference, 1942), nos. 14 and 2.

15 *Ibid.*

16 Jean-Yves Calvez, S.J., and Jacques Ferrin, S.J., *The Church and Social Justice,* (Chicago: Henry Regnery Company, 1961), pp. 36-51. See also Pius XII, *Address to Cardinals and Bishops,* November 2, 1954, AAS, 46, 672.

17 Pius XII. *Letter to Semaines Sociales* (France) 1952; cf. *America,* April 11, 1964, editorial page.

18 Senate Committee on Foreign Relations, *Possible Non-Military Scientific Developments and their Potential on Foreign Policy Problems of the United States,* (Washington, D. C., U. S. Government Printing Office, 1959), p. 30.

19 Daniel T. McColgan, *A Century of Charity,* (Milwaukee: Bruce Publishing Co., 1951), p. 252.

20 Seymour Martin Lipset, *Political Man,* (New York: Doubleday & Co., 1960).

21 Robert D. Cross, *op. cit.*, pp. 108-109.

22 *Ibid.*, p. 120.

23 Irving Shulman, *The Amboy Dukes*, (New York: Doubleday & Co.,

24 Paul VI, "Octogesima Adveniens," Apostolic Letter on the 80th Anniversary of "Rerum Novarum," May 15, 1971, *The Pope Speaks*, vol. 16, no. 2, 1971, p. 139.

25 *Ibid.*, pp. 140-146.

26 "Justice to the World," Recommendations by the 1971 Synod of Bishops, *The Pope Speaks*, vol. 16, no. 4 (1971), p. 377.

27 *Ibid.*, pp. 378-379.

28 Colin Clark, *Starvation or Plenty*, (New York: Taplinger Publishing Co., 1970), Foreword.

29 Pius XI, *op. cit.*, no. 127.

30 Lee Rainwater and William L. Yancey, *The Moynihan Report and the Politics of Controversy*, (Cambridge, Mass.: M.I.T. Press, 1967).

31 Paul VI, *op. cit.*, p. 382.

32 *The Church In Our Day*, Pastoral Statement of the Catholic Bishops of the United States, January 21, 1968 (Washington, D.C.: U.S. Catholic Conference, 1968) p. 24. See also John J. Dougherty, "A Voice for the Poor," *America*, February 28, 1968, pp. 252-253.

33 Richard M. Fagley, "The World Is Hungry," *America*, February 28, 1968, p. 250.

34 Mark R. Arnold, "The Good War that Might Have Been," *The New York Times Magazine*, September 29, 1974, p. 50.

35 Francis L. Broderick, *Right Reverend New Dealer: John A. Ryan*, (New York: The Macmillan Company, 1963), p. 74.

36 Max Weber, *The Protestant Ethic and the Spirit of Capitalism*, (translated by Talcott Parsons), (New York: Charles Scribner & Sons, 1958), pp. 13-27 for a good summary of this position.

37 Michael Harrington, *The Other American: Poverty in the United States*, (New York: Macmillan Company, 1962).

38 Joel F. Handler and Ellen Jane Hollingsworth, *The "Deserving Poor,"* (Chicago: Markham Publishing Company, 1971), p. ix.

39 Mark R. Arnold, *op. cit.*, p. 61.

40 John Cort, "The Evolution of a Catholic Worker," *Commonweal*, vol. XCIII, No. 14 January 8, 1971, p. 344.

41 1973 *Urban Internship Report*, United Parcel Service, New York, New York, p. 11. Available at 643 West 43rd Street, New York, New York 10036.

42 *Ibid.*, p. 12.

43 *Ibid.*, p. 15.

44. Robert D. Cross, op. cit., pp. 106-129, 206-224.

45 Gerhard Lenski, *The Religious Factor*, (New York: Doubleday & Co., 1961), pp. 89, 102, 131. 137-141.

46 Andrew M. Greeley and Peter H. Rossi, *The Education of Catholic Americans*, (New York: Doubleday & Co., Anchor Books, 1966), pp. 228.

47 Nathan Glazer and Daniel P. Moynihan, *Beyond the Melting Pot*, (Cambridge, Mass.: M.I.T. Press, 1970), p. LXIII.

48 Matthew Ahmann, "The Church and the Urban Negro," *America*, February 10, 1968, p. 181.

49 See Robert D. Cross, *ibid.*

50 John L. Thomas, *Religion and the American People*, (Westminster, Maryland: Newman Press, 1963), p. 257.

51 Abbe Michonneau, *Revolution in a City Parish*, (London: Blackfriars, 1949), p. 50.

52 22,500 parishes and missions
10,500 schools of all descriptions
1,500 institutions for orphans, delinquents, the sick and the aged.
See Catholic Directory 1974, P. J. Kenedy & Sons.

53 *Annual National Report* 1973, New York: Society of St. Vincent de Paul.

54 John L. Thomas, *op. cit.*, p. 261.

55 George A. Kelly, *Catholics and the Practice of the Faith 1967 and 1971*, (New York: St. John's University Press, 1972).

56 Robert J. Lampman, *op. cit.*, p. 166.

57 *Annual National Report 1973*, Society of St. Vincent de Paul.

58 *Ibid.*, p. 20.

59 Letter of Edward M. Kinney to George A. Kelly, September 30, 1974. Other data contained in the Report of the Executive Director to the Board of Trustees, Catholic Relief Services, U.S.C.C., 1974.

60 Winthrop S. Hudson, ed., *Religion in America*, (New York: Charles Scribner and Sons, 1973), p. 399.

61 John Cogley, *Catholic America* (New York: Dial Press, 1973), p. 93.

62 *Ibid.*

63 Robert Cross, *op. cit.*, p. 218.

64 This statement was first made by Cardinal Spellman on July 11, 1963 at the dedication of the Cornelius J. Drew Houses. Text is available from the Archives of the Archdiocese of New York (AANY) at St. Joseph's Seminary.

65 Available from the Archives of the Archdiocese of New York at St. Joseph's Seminary.

66 *The Lay Apostolate: Papal Teachings*, (Boston, Mass.: Daughters of St. Paul, 1961), no. 229.

67 *Ibid., October* 27, 1935, no. 602; See also Pius XII, January 25, 1950, no. 848.

68 John L. Thomas, *op. cit.*, p. 258.

69 Quoted in John Tracy Ellis, *The Life of James Cardinal Gibbons*, (Milwaukee: The Bruce Publishing Co., 1951), vol. II, p. 343N.

70 Pope Paul VI, *op. cit.*, (*Pope Speaks*, vol. 16, no. 2, 1971), p. 144.

71 Peter Berger, *The Invitation to Sociology*, (New York: Doubleday & Co., Anchor Books, 1963), p. 102.

72 *Statement of Policy and Programs*, The Citizens Crusade Against Poverty, New York City, October 13, 1964.

73 Kenneth Clark and Jeanette Hopkins, *A Relevant War Against Poverty*, (New York: Harper Torchbooks), 1969, p. 203.

74 *Ibid.*, p. 203-204.

75 Paul VI, *op. cit.*, p. 159.

76 Cf. *The Lay Apostolate*, nos. 664, 494, 653, 885.

77 *Ibid.*, no. 625, 578, 605, 1054, 239.

78 *Ibid.*, no. 919.

CHAPTER TWO

WHO ARE THE POOR WHO ARE ALWAYS WITH US?

*To the Question: " 'Can you draw me a composite of a poor
person?' I give the following answer. Surprisingly the first
ingredient is not black, but female. She will be non-white,
either black or Hispanic, over sixty-five, and not part of a
family unit. She will live in the rural South and because her
education is limited she will mainly be unemployed or em-
ployed only intermittently at the most marginal jobs that
just do not pay, such as plastics, which simply cannot compete with the price and quality of imports."*

NICHOLAS KISBURG
Legislative Director
Joint Council 16
International Brotherhood of Teamsters

The Question Itself

By the end of 1974 many Americans who call themselves middle class began to feel poorer, even those who could only make
Miami that winter, not Aruba, and certainly those who felt it
necessary to bypass the overdue new car or new suit. Mr. Inflation
started all of this with high prices for his consumer goods but
when he married Mrs. Recession for her stock in the unemployment business, the wrong people came to the wedding, the aged,
the sick, the dependent poor, the lower class unemployed, the
unemployable, and the young, mostly black youth, who ordinarily
would be learning to find their way through the labor market,
reaching for the first rung on their ladder of success. What might
have been another year of affluence became instead a time of
chronic complaining. Everybody blamed everyone else for what
went wrong at that wedding. The Republicans pointed the finger

to the guns and butter programs of the Great Society whose payment day was met with borrowed money and high prices. Democrats said the Republican need for a boom economy in 1972 to insure a large election victory flooded the country with the easy dollars which chased prices upward. Pacificists blamed the cost of the war in Vietnam. Nationalists explained the strain on the American pocketbook by the failure of Western Europe, Russia, China and Japan to pick up a fair share of the cost of feeding the Third World. Labor talked of multinational corporations, administered prices, exorbitant profits, while management named as chief villains an overfed inefficient government bureaucracy and a laboristic domination of the wage structure without compensating rises in productivity. Conservative economists faulted bankers for lending to people with inadequate collateral money which they in turn borrowed from someone else; liberal economists demanded more government spending and tax relief. The fight which radicals once defined in black and white terms now, as prosperous blacks were visible, was reclassified to set the have-nots of any color against all the haves. And when these scapegoats proved to be unsatisfactory redeemers for economic sinfulness, there were always the scoundrel Arabs, who apparently had outsmarted the American hucksters at their own special game of supply and demand.

All of which leaves Harry Truman's twenty-five-year-old question still unanswered. Who really talks for all the people? Choose your author or your vested interest and you can discover either reasonably well-satisfied workers content with the progress they have made or workers so bored and alienated that not even a union paycheck satisfies. Those old enough to remember the dog-eat-dog days of the depression may be grateful for their social security and medicare, even unemployment checks which sometimes run for a year, but a numerous lot seem to feel cheated by a system which does not give them more. So to get a good answer Flip Wilson may have to be re-edited and account taken of the probability that the answer you get is the answer you see before you ask. What you get is what you see.

The poor of the last decade may not have called for a war on poverty, at least not in the beginning (indeed there are those who think that the poor then had no understanding of poverty). But they are more assertive now.[1] In that earlier decade the social scientists, foundation experts and activists, prompted by LBJ's counsellors to put booming tax monies to work, may in fact have profited more from that effort than the poor. Yet as unsatisfactory to its generals as Vietnam was to the Pentagon, it did raise the consciousness of the citizenry to the fact that for all America's affluence poor people did exist, that they and the conditions which foster their plight should never be ignored. What to do about the problem then was another question and a much more difficult task, especially now that the upturns of the 1960's have been replaced by the most severe economic downturn of the post-war years. There is no doubt that the national economy is currently on a shake-down cruise of sorts, the end result of which is expected to be the elimination of those excessive imbalances—high government debt, high interest, high administered prices, high unproductive wage levels, high inventory, high budgets, high consumption, high political gambles and high hopes—which brought on the bloated health condition which always looked rosier than it was. Less than 2,000,000 people in March 1975 still remained without work after their unemployment checks ran out and prices especially of food-stuffs during the shake-up seem at last to be coming down, but the spectre of a long-term 8 or 9 percent unemployment rate beyond the legislated built in period of insurance payments conjures up nightmares of depression, even among those who only remember unemployed grandfathers. And granting the fear of feeding new inflation by federal pump-priming, the fact that the burdens will fall heavily on American youth and the established poor make for a major social problem.[2]

So when any time anyone asks these days "Who are the poor?", he can expect a fight if only because, no matter what the answer given, another side will question the credentials of the fellow who first decided who those poor are. Since a social situation is usually what people say it is, money-designated poor may not be the real poor. Some people do not feel poor because they have modest wants or they have a large ability to make ends meet. Consequently, the expert who presumes with final authority to answer the question can expect more than one hostile confrontation, which probably explains why Nathan Glazer, "Gave up the claim to know how to answer."[3] The end result is that the battle between the optimists and the pessimists rages on.[4]

The problem for Catholics, who must eventually choose their own answer to the question, is to make sure they have a good grasp of the data and a sense of the varying perspectives within which the data can be interpreted. Historically, we have been criticized as being high on moralisms and short on facts, too friendly or too hostile to business, labor or government. And unquestionably, because the controlling Protestant establishment was blind to the Catholic and Jewish poor, we tended to be severe critics of the status quo.

But there is a new situation facing American Catholics. The tenor of the present American times is to be anti-establishment across the board, against the American system, against organized labor as well as business, a mass mind which has been created by contemporary intellectuals and supported politically by those still not fully the beneficiaries of general American prosperity. The distrust of anything American is most acutely expressed by the spokesmen of the Third World most of whom are committed socialists. In fact the socialist ethos dominates the thinking even of some leading American intellectuals, who usually and virulently distrust government as something evil—except in economic matters. This socialist ethos has a rhetoric flowing out of its common assumptions, the chief of which is that there is plenty of wealth around if only it is properly distributed. The validity of this assumption is reinforced by repeated assertions that American affluence is a deplorable condition of life (as the poor are guaranteed a share in it), repeated denials that conditions are improving (as the automobiles in the ghetto continue to double park) and that the only thing needed to uplift the poor is another piece of social legislation. Mention is rarely made by these rhetoricians that while the American poor have some reason to complain, they are better off here than anywhere else in the world, or that the working class is far more content with their lot than the more affluent intellectuals. It is almost heresy to indicate that many of the problems of the poor in countries like India are due not to population size, nor to exploiters but to its own economic incompetence, or to the fact that Britain, socialized for twenty-five years, today owns a lesser share of the gross international product than it had in 1947, that its government has not redistributed its wealth any better, nor are the British people comparatively more prosperous than they were then.

Some commentators are beginning to strike back at this acquiescence by American spokesmen to the allegations which make the socialist myth credible, probably because for too long they have been made to feel guilty themselves about being so prosperous while so many poor live elsewhere. Daniel Moynihan, who recently returned from India after completing a tour of duty as American ambassador, is one such debunker. Apparently he is sick and tired of such induced guilt feelings. To the problems of poverty his answer is wealth production, not wealth redistribution. The size of the pie is what counts. When the bottom share is $5,000 and not $100 nor $500, people know the difference. Countries which improve their wealth production also improve the lot of their people. Nonproducers do not and consistently the record shows that the socialist countries set on ideological equality more than growing enterprise end up as poor wealth producers, equalizing only lower living standards. Moynihan suggests:

> It is time we asserted that inequalities in the world may not be so much a matter of condition as of performance.[5]

Outspokenly blunt about the naivete of Americans who have allowed their culture to move toward a depreciation of hard work and discipline, an overexaggeration of the value of free-flowing food and money to the poor, he concludes,

> It is past time we ceased to apologize for our imperfect democracy. Find its equal.[6]

The oft-repeated cliche that Catholics in the United States

tend to adapt new articles of a social creed just about when everyone else is about to give them up (capitalism and patriotism are
good examples) may take on new flesh and blood as a result of
two answers to the American poverty problem in the U.S.
Catholic Conference, the staff arm of the American bishops. Within
a few months of each other early in 1975, the USCC produced a
booklet entitled *Liberty and Justice for All,* ostensibly the Church's
contribution to the celebration of the country's bicentennial, and
Poverty in American Democracy: A Study of Social Power, a study
done by the bishop-sponsored Campaign for Human Development,
to which American Catholics contribute seven million dollars annually.[7] Each of these booklets is central not so much to the question "Who are the poor?" as to the perspective within which one
seeks a proper answer in order that remedies provide more than
verbal promise. In general both booklets by devoting most space
to the negative aspects of the American condition seem to suggest
that heavy doses of social criticism and radical social action are
the preferred therapy for problems of American poverty. Andrew
Greeley is particularly incensed by *Liberty and Justice For All*
primarily because the fact that the American standard of living had
doubled within twenty years, that more minorities have come to
enjoy the abundant life, that one quarter of the world's population
have been fed by hundreds of billions of dollars of the hard-earned
money of American workers, have been completely ignored. He
wrote the booklet off as

a bitter and sometimes violent attack on American society.

a shabby, shameful, and disgraceful attack on the American
people.

a product of the liberal wing of the American hierarchy.[8]

Poverty in American Democracy, a serious and well-done effort
to capsulate the data associated with the money income, social
services, and political influence available to the poor, is also written from one side of the proposed answer.[9] The assumption of this

approach is that poverty is the result simply of the mal-distribution of existing abundant wealth and that there is some horrible and sinister story underlying the fact that "virtually the same distribution (of income) as existed in 1969 has existed for the last sixty years."[10] The common tendency of radicals to define as "rich" anyone who earns $20,000 annually and as "poor" anyone with less than $10,000 a year[11] is partly reflected in this book when the author, analyzing income distribution, changes the traditional government classification of "top fifth" to read "richest fifth," without noting that people who enter that fifth earn $17,500 and are not likely to read themselves as rich.[12]

1960 *America Ten Years Later*

By confessional conviction Catholic social actionists working for the poor can follow any political program as long as they are committed to the poor and contributing to their uplift. Neither prayer, fasting, nor radicalism are by themselves the endorsed methodology, although all are required in given situations. But all Catholics ought to look at the facts and decide for themselves what they mean, which brings us back to the initial question: Who are the poor? In answering this question it seems best to look backward at general trends discoverable from actual census data covering the nation than to rely on up-to-the-minute sample estimates, which usually are modified by the analyses of data deriving from subsequent door-to-door head counts. (The 1980 census will be a better vantage point from which to judge current problems.)

The Bureau of the Census made a beginning of an answer with the announcement that in 1971 a non-farm family of four needed $4,137 to live *above* its defined poverty level. By that standard alone 25,600,000 Americans were catalogued as living in poverty.[13] But since Gallup Pollsters reported in 1972 that people themselves said $8,000 was the basic living level for a family of four, who could survive on less than $5,000? Even at the higher level some 19,000,000 families (70,000,000 Americans) or one-third of all Americans, can stake their claim to the name "poor." To compound the dilemma of definition another Gallup poll in the same year reported that blacks more than whites thought the life in America was improving.

Statistics, therefore, are perilous norms for human judgment, partly because the only universally applicable data are derived from census reports, which are at best controversial.[14] University studies may suggest particular hypotheses. But despite their short-comings only federal data blanketing the total population offers a national or regional view of affluence or its lack. The special problem is that, even the most sophisticated statisticians reading the tables, appear to have their own special ideological or class commitments. Yet, unless some data are presented as "provable facts," no discussion is possible. With these caveats, the following elemental "facts" are presented as a partial answer to the question: Who are the poor?

Fact One—A labor force of 90 million workers feed, clothe, and shelter 200 million Americans. Sixty percent of these workers are men. In the urban areas, where most virulent controversies over poverty occur, white families outnumber black families 37 to 4 million.

Fact Two—The median income* (1971) was one third higher for whites than for blacks. Said differently, annual black family income in 1971 was only 63 percent of white income, although when the black family was headed by a male, the family propor-tion rose to 76 percent.

	All Families	Male-Headed	Female-Headed
White	$10,671	$11,143	$5,842
Black	$ 6,714	$ 8,067	$3,645

Fact Three—The median income of black families is nearer to parity with whites, only if there are two or more wage earners.

	One Earner	Two Earners
White	$9,173	$11,973
Black	$5,330	$ 9,041

---

*A median figure is one which divides a group in two. Fifty percent of the group is found above and below the indicated figure.

Fact Four—The largest proportion of low-income people are black women.

	Male	Female	White	Black
		Proportions in Each Category		
Under $7,000	25.0	65.8	27.0	54.0
$7,000 up to $10,000	18.9	16.0	18.6	18.3
$10,000 up to $15,000	28.9	11.9	28.0	17.2
$15,000 up to $25,000	21.4	5.4	20.6	9.5
$25,000 and over	5.9	.9	5.8	1.1

Fact Five—Eighty percent of all American families, white or black, average less than $15,000 a year.

Percentiles	Average 1971 Income
Lowest 20 percent	$ 3,247
Second Fifth	7,025
Third Fifth	10,272
Fourth Fifth	13,991
Top 20 percent	24,559

Fact Six—The economic level of urban blacks vis-a-vis whites has improved in the decade 1960-1970. The proportions shifting from lower to higher income levels are larger for blacks than for whites.

	Whites		Blacks	
		Proportion at Each Level		
Family Income	1960	1970	1960	1970
Under $8,000	34.9 down to 31.8		89.1 down to 58.7	
$8,000 up to $15,000	41.7 up to	43.2	10.0 up to	31.0
$15,000 up to $25,000	18.0 up to	19.2	0.8 up to	8.9
$25,000 and over	5.3 up to	5.8	0.2 up to	1.5

Fact Seven—The Census Bureau by definition counts 25,600,000 Americans (one out of eight) below the poverty level. The largest *numbers* of these are whites, especially women, under 22 years of age, living in central cities and the South. The largest *proportions* are members of the black community, especially women.

Millions Below the Poverty Level

Age		Race	
Under 22	12.4M	White	17.8 (one out of ten whites)
22-64	8.9M	Black	7.8 (one out of three blacks)

		North and West		South	
Residence		White	Black	White	Black
Central City	8.9	11.5	2.6	6.3	4.8
Suburbia	5.6				

Male Headed Families		Female Headed Families	
White	Black	White	Black
10.6	3.5	7.1	4.3

Fact Eight—Unemployment rates for blacks in 1972 were double that for whites in all age groups and sexes, even though rates vary with age, education, and length of unemployment. Although the national unemployment average in 1972 was 5.6, the unemployed rate beyond fifteen weeks (the period covered by unemployment insurance) was only 1.3.

Rates of Unemployment

By Age of Male Workers				By Age of Female Workers			
Under 20		Over 20		Under 20		Over 20	
Whites	Blacks	Whites	Blacks	Whites	Blacks	Whites	Blacks
14.2	29.7	3.6	6.8	14.2	38.5	4.9	8.8

By Education of Worker

	White	Black
Under Twelve Years....	6.6	10.6
12 Years	5.1	9.6
More than 12	3.5	6.5

The American Value System

An examination of these data suggest that the question: Who are the poor? cannot be answered in absolute terms. By the absolute standards of this country or any other, there are relatively few poor in the United States. No one, save a thoroughly disorganized human being need sleep outdoors or under bridges, as they do in civilized France. Food on American Boweries is not prepared by a Delmonico chef, but thousands stay alive there.

Nonetheless, millions of American families are poor in their own eyes. When, therefore, there is talk in the United States about poverty, it is talk about families or individuals who have much less income than most others. When we talk about giving more to the poor, we mean reducing inequalities, usually as a result of the redistribution of income. And that means taking from those who have more. If poverty is seen in racial terms, it means taking from whites and giving to blacks. If it is seen in sexual terms, it means taking from men and giving to women. Thomas Merton did not make the sociological determination of the poverty base but he did sense what was the question's spiritual significance.

> It is easy to tell the poor to accept their poverty as God's will when you yourself have warm clothes and plenty of food and medical care and a roof over your head and no worry about the rent. But if you want them to believe you, try to share some of their poverty and see if you can accept it as God's will yourself.[15]

This still leaves us with the sociological question: What is the cut-off point between the haves and the have-nots? Someone must determine who are those who have too much to be shared with those who have too little. Culture plays a part here. Judgments about poverty change from country to country, from decade to decade. During a gasoline shortage Britons manage to keep a stiff upper lip in the absence of pence or petrol which costs two dollars a gallon. Americans, even in the ghetto, consider themselves disadvantaged if perforce they must wait in line for gas which is available and costs the better part of one dollar per gallon. People's expectations, therefore, are very germane to the measurement of the poverty level. The poor are sometimes poor in America because their expectations outreach their purchasing power. The typical middle American, which means almost everybody, measures his family needs in terms of a gracious home, stereo or certainly television, and some decencies like good scotch or a winter holiday. The poor American dreams his own dreams and it may include weekend block-parties, a summer bungalow, or a cheap station wagon. There are many frills to American life which not even the poor associate with affluence. So before one asks about the meanings and levels of poverty, a look at the extent of affluence in the United States is appropriate.

It is one of our better kept secrets that genuine affluence exists in America only at the top of the economic pinnacle. Hundreds of Americans earn a million dollars a year annually but the average income in 1971 for the top five percent of the labor force was $38,000. The Rockefellers, the Harrimans, the Kennedys enjoy the benefit of extraordinary inherited resources and extraordinary earned income. But the less understood fact is that the fight for a proper share of the gross national product is a daily grind for the rest of the population, producers, sellers and wage earners alike. And most available data fail to give proper weight to the cost of educating children, particularly if more than two are involved or if their education is not subsidized by tax monies.

Indeed the American economy might more aptly be described as hard working rather than affluent. Only 432,000 families—out of 54,373,000—earned more than $50,000 in 1972. The president of General Motors received a salary almost running into seven figures, but the average income of his peers, the top economic group in the country, was $70,000, a third of which was eaten up by city, state, and federal taxes. And what is true of lower classes is also true here: the majority of these affluent families had two and three wage earners.

The families of middle-management, national labor leaders, university full-professors and high school principals—those who earned between $25,000 and $50,000 in 1972—totalled 3,500,000, less than 7 percent of the labor force. Three quarters of these families had two wage earners, and one-third was supported by three working members. The same condition of multiple workers characterizes the life-style of the so-called middle class, that group which earned between $15,000 and $25,000. Hardly any union member or experienced white-collar worker lacks membership in this group of 12,500,000 families.[16]

It is facts like these which must be faced by those talking about money redistribution. Ninety-three out of every 100 Americans earn less than $25,000. Not even a statistical "one" earns more than $50,000, and only seven of that 100 earn $25,000. Thirty earned $15,000 and an additional fifteen wage earners took home $12,000 in 1972. Debaters argue that 11,000,000 families at the top made more money than the next 33,000,000 families but fail to mention that membership in the top fifth of the American working elite begins at $17,760. Union members (bricklayers and hod carriers; civil servants—the cops, firemen and teachers) are incredulous when they are told that they belong to the wealthiest fifth of the country.

If these legal figures are true, then middle class members with their feeding problems ought to be more understanding of the plight of welfare mothers than they really are. On the kind of money they are reported to have, neither class can really make it. It is just possible, and not at all unlikely, that both middle class and poor alike have illegal incomes. How else do they survive the supermarket? But guesses about illegal income are no help to a discussion of the poverty problem.

What these data do suggest, however, is that the possible range of redistribution is quite limited, for the simple reason that there is not much to take away because there are not that many haves. Experts look at the trillion dollar national income and think maybe one per cent—$10,000,000,000—could be moved around. That means taking $500 each from the $50,000 men or a total of $216,000,000 which would not wipe out the projected budget deficit of New York City for 1975. Only Marxist demagogues or hungry politicians out of power (those "in" have some sense) talk any more about dismantling vast fortunes. When the upper strata of American society are examined, they turn out to have not just millionaires with swollen incomes[17] but teachers, shopkeepers, professional and technical workers, even truck drivers. Who is going to confiscate their hard earned money? The people down the economic line obviously do not eat or drink as well as union truck drivers and rightfully want what the truck driver has. The truck driver has his own answer to the poor: "Let 'em work." But the truck driver is wrong too. Work by itself does not keep people from being poor. The federal government places 1,500,000 black families below the poverty level. But 40 percent of that number had one wage earner, 15 percent had two, 6 percent had three, so that all that working did not help 1,000,000 black families raise themselves over and beyond the federal poverty line.[18]

People are inclined to forget that anyone earning a minimum wage of two dollars an hour has an annual income of $4,000 before taxes. Add a wife and two children and you have the poverty level, especially if the family is Catholic and believes that the poor have a right to be born.

Several facts, therefore, are indisputable.

1. The median money income of an American family has nearly tripled in the last twenty years.
2. More families enjoy not only the benefits of higher family income but an upgraded standard of living. In 1952 one out of twenty Americans earned $15,000 or more; by 1972 six did. For every ten earning less than $4,000 in 1952, only six were at that level twenty years later.
3. The increase in income levels is due mainly to multiple wage earners in the family, mostly to the return of wives to the active labor market.
4. The annual rate of growth in the mean income of black families (6.1 percent) was higher than for white families (5.2 percent).

But what about the ten billion dollars which economists say can be moved toward the have-nots? Three things can be said. First, this will pay the costs for two months of any new program of socialized medicine. Secondly, it may not go where hopefuls think it ought. Pressure exerted by well-meaning people in favor of blacks, forget that two-thirds of the 25.6 million persons below the poverty level are white. The political problems are tremendous. One-third of all blacks are in poverty, almost too much for any single group to bear, be they Chicanos, Catholics, Chicagoans or blacks. But the economic pie is never divided by slide rule. Thirdly, public opinion is likely to give ten billion to many causes, only one of which will be the poor. Regardless of facts, politicized society tends to deal only with *case poverty,* i.e., the poor family with a junk filled yard and a drunken father. When public money is disbursed for poverty it usually is to cases of mental deficiency, bad health, undisciplined sexuality, alcohol or ignorance.

The Black Family

Major opinion-makers are comfortable with the progress of the black family. As families, blacks moved closer to income parity with the white middle class. This is especially true of black families in the North and Western part of the country, where husband and wife both work, and quite likely if they are under thirty-five years of age. Geography, like sex, is at times more relevant to the poverty question than race, which explains why Southern whites do not do as well as their Northern brothers, black or white. There is a political problem connected with these assertions. Some think that any suggestion of substantial progress within the last fifteen years, especially by blacks, will be injurious to further upward movement. Even though there is little chance that voting rights, equal educational or job opportunities, are likely to be reversed by anyone ever, rhetoricians insist on denying improvement, while demagogues maintain that the condition of the "Lumpenproletariat" is really worse.

Ben J. Wattenberg and Richard Scammon, former officials of the federal government,[19] in 1973 decried the blanket of silence which has enveloped the socio-economic advances of the poor since 1960. The studious efforts made to deny these advances, the more astounding claim that blacks are far worse off now than they were ten years ago, are dismissed by them as incredible.[20] The situation of the poor, especially the black, is not universally good, nor do blacks yet have general economic parity with whites, nor is poverty in the United States a thing of the past, according to Wattenberg-Scammon. But they insist:

The image of the black in America must be changed, from an earlier one of an uneducated, unemployed, poverty-stricken slum-dweller, to that of an individual earning a living wage at a decent job, with children who stay in school, and aspire to still better wages and still better jobs, in a decent if unelaborate dwelling, still economically behind his white counterpart but catching up.[21]

They stress the progress theme for two good reasons: (1) If the majority of American blacks continue to be painted as ever unending stereotypes of human misery and degradation "it simply makes no sense to demand of white middle-class Americans that they welcome (such types) into their neighborhoods, schools, or places of work;" and (2) continued pessimistic portrayals will incline middle class voters, including many middle class blacks, to refuse social payments for families whom they believe are constitutionally "shiftless."[22]

However much the concept "middle class" is denigrated, the term in the mind of the poor means three square meals a day, decent clothing, sanitary housing, safe neighborhoods, good schools, perhaps a college education for the children. Wattenberg and Scammon believe that the poor, especially blacks, have made much headway toward satisfying the basic desires. The reasons in support of this judgment are four:

1. While black income in 1971 was still only two-thirds of white income, the improvement is significant because fifteen years ago it was less than half of white income. In the North black income is 74 percent of white income. If the income of married couples is compared black income is 88 percent of white.

2. The drop in unemployment rates has been sharper for blacks than for whites. Whereas in 1962 for very 250 blacks unemployed 100 whites were so deprived. Ten years later the ratio was 170:100, not exactly parity, but substantial improvement.

3. Within the same period proportionately three times as

many blacks moved into middle-class occupations (white-collar workers, craftsmen, operatives) as whites.
4. While the percentage of blacks on welfare has increased (primarily because poor blacks are receiving better service), the percentage of blacks in poverty has gone down from 48 to 29 percent in the last twelve years.

While the economic and social gap separating whites and blacks is still a national disgrace, Wattenberg-Scammon conclude:

In a society that prides itself on being middle class, blacks are now moving into the middle class in unprecedented numbers. In a society that scorns the high school drop-out and offers work to the high school graduate, blacks are now finishing high school and significant numbers are going on to college. In a culture that has a clear idea of what is a good job and what is not, blacks are now moving into good jobs.[23]

The critics of these optimistic conclusions are not few and not always friendly.[24] They charge that blacks are still undereducated and underemployed, still cannot join craft unions, that improved income is mostly due to black women working all year round and for longer hours, that even the measurable gains under the Johnson administration have reached a plateau and can be reversed. Yet it looks like the biggest problem facing blacks in the urban area is by their own testimony no longer unemployment but crime.[25]

White Poverty

There is another poor about whom not much is known. Recent studies indicate that many aged ethnics live in abject poverty, that many of their sons do not earn middle class incomes, and their grandsons are as alienated as anyone else. But because scholars, journalists, and social reformers give them little attention, the precise number and composition of the white poverty class are no more precise than educated guesses. When these white ethnics are not called racists, they are ignored—by social agencies and programs designed to deal with the culture of poverty. Part of the reasons for this neglect is that society has come to expect them to take care of themselves. And in large measure they do because their neighborhoods are usually stable units in an otherwise unstable world. In the single language ghetto many thousands find not only their haven but their identity. And since most of these communities are Catholic, these particular poor tend to cluster around the Church, as the poor Jews cluster around their synagogue. But these poor can be the bridge to racial harmony, precisely because they are poor and white, not likely to be marched around, certainly not trampled upon even by other poor. The poor whites number perhaps 18,000,000 and will have their hand out for any contemplated redistribution.

Who Then Are The Poor?

Many millions who are and those who think they are. Blacks certainly, but mostly white, the very young and the very old, Southerners more than Yankees. The statistical measure cannot tell the whole story, nor do scholars have the last word.

The testimony of one's own eyes witness the conditions, almost as well as scholarship. Black faces acting on the athletic field and dramatic stage, or cavorting through a peppy Colgate commercial are only a few signs of the times. Black cops, black firemen, black bus drivers, black teachers, black construction men are where they were not ten years ago. Blacks may be or may not be living in the white man's house or street, but "whitey" knows where $50,000 homes are now occupied by blacks. Few people know that there are now 2,500 black elected officials holding office across the country, but they do know that their racial options in the voting booth are quite wide. Any white shopper in poverty areas sees for himself that the cart pushed by the black man is no less packed than his own. Indeed, the "Southern gentleman" currently is seeing more substantial change right now than any other American.[26]

Crisis strategists may still complain that the $5,000 black who at one time was $5,000 behind the white earning $10,000, is now $10,000 behind him, even though both have moved to $40,000-$50,000 levels respectively. Yet though large residues of discrimination continue against blacks, detached onlookers accept and applaud the achievements of the past decade and attribute the shift of real income to blacks to the more important "shift in opportunity."[27]

The good will of the white population had little to do with this improvement. The major lesson for policy makers and public is that social advancement came as a result of the ongoing bullishness of the American economy. It is an old maxim of economics that blacks fare better in prosperity than in recession or depression. Under conditions of recession unemployment for blacks will rise proportionately more than for whites. But new things have occurred to suggest that the traditional pattern of "last hired-first fired" for blacks has already been altered. Curtis Gilroy, an economist working for the Bureau of Labor Statistics, states the change as follows:

> The phenomenon of blacks being more adversely affected than whites by business downturns has been mitigated over the last several business cycles. For every successive peak-to-trough period, black workers have shared less of the increase in unemployment. In the 1957-58 downturn, for example, proportionate to the size of the labor force, 20 black workers were added to the unemployment totals for every 10 white workers; however, during the 1969-70 recession, only 14 blacks became jobless for every 10 white workers. Moreover, proportionately more blacks than whites have left the ranks of the unemployed with each successive recovery period. During the 1954-57 recovery, 13 black workers for every 10 white workers left the unemployed ranks, while in the 1961-69 period of prosperity, there was a decrease of 22 unemployed black workers for every 10 white workers.[28]

Progress in dealing with poverty must be sought in a prosperous economy for everyone, in the proverbial larger pie. It cannot be measured in terms of the other fellow. To speak of poverty in black terms or Spanish terms is to create resistance in the larger numbers of whites who live with poverty too. The narrower the perception of the problem, the more likely it will be associated with individual failure, of itself the usual reason why society disclaims responsibility. And society—private and public—is essential. Without some kind of a "Great Society" the problem will never be licked. The great progress made by the poor of all races during the 1960-1972 period can be attributed to the impulses of social pressures and social legislation. If the 1974-1975 recession can be laid at the door of a government who for victory on election day deferred paying for expensive programs rather than tax, the gains nonetheless are real and cannot be negated. For one thing the Civil Rights Act of 1964 has given blacks political power they never enjoyed before, a power which as a matter of fact transcends anything held by women or the aged.

The politics of belittling progress can be just as dangerous as the politics of inciting unrealistic and excessive expectations. It is also as immoral as the politics of benign neglect. Progress comes only through the ebb and flow of conflict and cooperation between classes, races and ethnic or religious groups. Too much consistent conflict, failure to work out cooperative developments, leads eventually to further depressions of real income, as of spirit. When politically inculcated pessimism becomes the rule of the day, the young have little reason to plan their future because they have been told there is no future.

The real lesson of the last ten years is that "making it" results from the intense desire of the poor to "make it," as it results from any other factor. People will pour out energy and sacrifice as long as they have hope, encouragement, and a little patience. Costs of "making it" will always be high. Blacks, for example, earn less per hour, less per week. Black wives work longer hours, hold full-time jobs all year, year after year, while white wives work shorter hours, part time, and frequently suspend work. The actual median take-home pay for blacks in many areas is less than weekly welfare allotments. But as long as they see rays of hope and inches of progress, the contemporary poor are likely to imitate, rather than fall short of, the advances made by earlier ethnic groups. The bearish economy of the past two years—inflationary prices, rising rates of unemployment, falling Dow-Jones averages, loss of public confidence in government, business, labor—has made economic life harder for everyone, save the upper-upper class, and has burdened mostly the poor. But by comparison with other citizens in the western world, Americans still enjoy visible prosperity, and considering the resiliency of this economy, the cyclical movement of the past generation towards more equitable sharing of produced wealth is certain to continue. The gross national product which in 1975 will reach $1,500,000,000 is expected to grow by another one trillion dollars in 1980 with personal income growing proportionately. But not everyone will be happy even with this unprecedented growth, because the accent up and down the line is likely still to be "more."

NOTES FOR CHAPTER TWO

1 See Richard W. Poston, *The Gang and the Establishment,* (New York, Harper and Row, 1971), pp. 201-2. See also Daniel P. Moynihan, *Maximum Feasible Misunderstanding: Community Action in the War on Poverty,* (New York, Free Press, 1970), pp. 188-189. Moynihan's thesis is that the social scientists did not know as much as they thought they did or as government officials thought they did. Theories plausible in the academic world did not work out significantly in radically altering the poverty picture. Indeed in his latest book *The Politics of Guaranteed Income: The Nixon Administration and the Family Assistance Plan* (New York, Random House, 1973), p. 87, Moynihan argues that political naivete flowing out of a doctrinaire approach to reality prevented more being done for the poor. Only a piecemeal approach that costs realistic prices is ever politically possible. But ideologues continue to insist as much for uplift for New York as for Mississippi, even though welfare benefits in New York are higher than anything that can be devised for a national program.

2 See some projections in a report of the *New York Times,* March 8, 1975, p. 1.

3 Nathan Glazer, "Ethnicity and the School," *Commentary,* vol. 58, no. 3, September, 1974, p. 58.

4 See an editorial entitled precisely that, "Optimists vs. Pessimists," in *America,* February 22, 1975.

5 Daniel P. Moynihan, "The United States in Opposition," *Commentary,* vol. 59, no. 3, March 1975, p. 42.

6 *Ibid.,* p. 43.

7　Each of these are avaliable from the United States Catholic Conference, 1312 Massachusetts Avenue, N.W., Washington, D. C. 20005.

8　Andrew Greeley, "Social Activism—Real or Rad/Chic?" *National Catholic Reporter*, February 7, 1975, p. 8. See *National Catholic Reporter*, February 28, 1975, p. 11. One priest participant in seminars conducted by USCC to develop a consensus for this booklet also objected to the final product, which he alleges is unrepresentative.

9　A perusal of some of the chapters might lead a reader to conclude that we in America lived in Dickensonian England. No general description of American economic life is presented, no stress on progress but much on the powerlessness and abuse of the poor (ch. 3). The American ethos is identified with materialism and discrimination (ch. 4), the unhappiness of workers, the crookedness of the wealthy (ch. 5), the maldistribution of wealth and power in the United States (ch. 6), identification of the Church with power to the poor (ch. 7). Nothing in the book really tells the story of organized labor's contribution to worker well-being. Although about a third of the book tells how American corporations hurt the poor, little is said of complaints of the poor against trade unions. The present welfare system apparently is beyond all criticism, although the Woodrow Wilson of 1911 is dragged in as a critic of the American middle class, as if the middle class of 1911 is what is still with us. The unsuspecting reader also has no idea that some authorities cited (such as Frances Piven and Richard Cloward) are radical social critics with a radical slant on reality and unlimited confidence in social activism as *the* answer to poverty.

10　*Ibid.*, p. 100.

11　See the complaint of the conservative *National Review* (February 28, 1975, p. 207) against such labellings finding their way into government documents.

12　See an editorial in *Commonweal*, February 28, 1975, page 411, sympathetic to the general approach of the book.

13　*Social Indicators 1973*, Washington: U.S. Government Printing Office, 1973, pp. 173, 183.

14　The two government studies with 1971 data, unless otherwise indicated, which will be used in this study are *Social Indicators*, pp. 140ff. and *General Social and Economic Characteristics*: (hereafter called *General Characteristics*), First Report, Census of Population, 1970, Washington, D.C., U. S. Government Printing Office, 1972 pp. 377 ff.

15　Thomas Merton, *New Seeds of Contemplation*, (London: Burns and Oates, 1961), p. 139.

16　U. S. Bureau of the Census, *Current Population Report*, Series 8-60, No. 90, "Money Income in 1972 of Families and Persons in the United States," U.S. Government Printing Office, Washington, D.C., 1973, p. 48ff.

17　See a book by Robert Halburner, *An Inquiry Into the Human Prospect.*

18 *Current Population Report,* p. 3-5.

19 These men are co-authors of *This USA,* (Garden City: Doubleday, 1965) and *The Real Majority,* (New York: Coward-McCann, 1971). Wattenberg, as an aid to President Johnson, was instrumental in the publication by the government of the "Social and Economic Conditions of Negroes in the United States," 1967 and 1968; Scammon has been Director of the Census Bureau and a consultant of the Civil Rights Commission.

20 Ben J. Wattenberg and Richard M. Scammon, "Black Progress and Liberal Rhetoric," *Commentary,* vol. 55, no. 4, April, 1973, pp. 35-44.

21 *Ibid.,* p. 38.

22 *Ibid.,* pp. 39, 44.

23 *Ibid.,* p. 41.

24 Letters from Readers: "On the Nature of Black Progress," *Commentary,* vol. 56, no. 2, pp. 4-22.

25 The Harris Pollsters discovered in Harlem that when asked "What are two or three of the biggest problems facing people such as yourself?" the blacks made crime, housing, drugs, dirty streets their biggest problems, which is precisely how the whites and the Spanish answered the question. *New York Times,* November 21, 1974, p. 49.

26 *U. S. News and World Report,* February 25, 1974, p. 56.

27 Robert M. Hauser and David L. Featherman, "Socioeconomic Achievements of U.S. Men, 1962 to 1972," *Science,* vol. 185, no. 4148, July 26, 1974, pp. 325-328.

28 Curtis L. Gilroy, "Black and White Unemployment: The Dynamics of the Differential," *Monthly Labor Review,* vol. 97, no. 2, February, 1974, p. 42.

CHAPTER THREE

THE LORD HELPS THOSE WHO HELP THEMSELVES

"I had always been close to the Church and to many good priests. But when we started our strike in Delano I was shocked. We could not have a meeting of farm workers in any of the halls owned by the Church. The local growers were very much involved in the Catholic schools. As a matter of fact I was politely asked to remove my children from the schools because the growers did not like my children going to school with their children. The last time I went to service in a Church was during that strike. We had no food to eat except what people gave us and a Catholic priest went around asking people to go back to work."

MRS. DOLORES HUERTA
United Farm Workers of America

The Paradox of Our Time

A certain insanity is abroad in the world. Men of violence call themselves men of peace. Terminating a life unborn or too long born is a matter of high principle for the man of progress. To raid a political rival's filing cabinet is a high crime but stealing classified government documents is an act of civic virtue. Proponents of the sanctity of the free market meet secretly to drive competitors out of business. In a land which lives by the offhand dictum of Samuel Gompers, "I want more," it is temerarious to suggest that those who have more take less. And the Church which tells its people that they cannot enter the Kingdom unless they do for others, is forced by reality to remind others that the Lord only helps those who help themselves.

As the controversy in the Church over *Humanae Vitae* clearly demonstrated, the disorientation of our time is moral, not psychological. Commitment to poverty in spirit and to the poor no longer is associated with cross-carrying or self-denial or giving up. That went out with the Lenten Fast. Presidents and bishops still ask for restraint in wage demands, profits or the use of energy, but such calls to penance are out of fashion in a culture which believes that everyone is entitled to get his now.

This paradox of our time is a stumbling block to any redistribution of income which benefits the poor. The economic pot of any nation is only so large. Assertions that movement into the middle class can be accompanied by taking away the yachts or Cadillacs of the economic royalists are no longer believable. If ten billion dollars were issued tomorrow in hard cash, everyone below the poverty line would receive $400 this year. As a result, the poor would henceforth live on the royal sum of twelve dollars a day instead of the eleven they currently have. Under the best of circumstances this is not a happy prospect. It is less than happy if the dominant social force is "more." While Dorothy Day is the proper symbolic figure for those willing to take less so that more is available for sharing, Samuel Gompers is the more likely leader of the masses, even of those who do not like his trade unions.

Reformers continue to insist that, when the lower ten percent share only two percent of national income, while the upper tenth enjoy twenty percent, money must be moved around. That is somewhat possible when the economy is producing new goods, new services and, therefore, new money. But even when new money is available, everyone up and down the line has his hand out. If the productivity increase is two percent, the $15,000 a year man wants two percent more because he helped make the increase. The $30,000 man feels the same way. And whether organized or unorganized, all workers have a way of limiting their productivity so that if they do not profit, no one does. Government can create all the "make work projects" it wants (now called "rip off jobs") but these have temporary value and serve only a few. Lyndon Johnson once had the ideal solution: make everyone prosperous without taking anything away from anyone. Unfortunately he did it on borrowed money. And when the moment came to pay his debts, the belt of government spending was tightened, new projects were cancelled, people were laid off. Even if Johnson found the secret, so that everybody worked, there was no unemployment and a plentiful supply of money, we would soon be back in trouble. People with money always want more. They drive prices higher and higher. The real value of the dollar declines, investors are slow to chance the market, manufacturers cut-back on production, people are laid off, prices begin to tumble and the cycle of recession returns.

The conclusion seems obvious: improvement in the lot of the poor depends on an ever expanding economy. People must become more productive because either new technology or hard work turns out more products which people can buy at a fair price because they have the money. Too much money in the wrong place bids prices higher, drives inefficient operators out of business, and starts the business cycle on its merry way to a new wave of ups and downs. The only certain lesson of the uncertain economic science is that people together earn only the value of the product they create. A percentage of that value can be moved around but very slowly. "Make work" employment at best is a band-aid for the poor. No one can "make" five million "no social value" jobs nor "make" money to pay all their salaries.

There Is No Magic

The uplift of the poor is a complicated task which is why professional problem-solvers tend to throw up their hands, especially if they look at poverty only in statistical terms. On the other hand, those who see the problem solely in personal terms, who make the poor "our" problem, will need several eternities before all the poor can be reached, let alone uplifted.

Movement out of poverty, then, comes not so much because it is engineered but more likely through personal industry and self-help organizations. The day of *noblesse oblige* is over. No longer can one expect to receive benefits from on high simply because they are owed. Saints give away advantages because it is the thing they do best. The nobility of God's presence impels them to give the coat with the shoes, to walk two miles when one will do just enough. The poor sometimes with nothing to give but themselves have that kind of saintly nobility. But *noblesse oblige* works only when people are better than they really are.

The capitalists are more realistic. They take people as they are likely to be, at their worst if necessary. Moneymakers prefer to work by contract on profitable terms. The contract is not really an ideal relationship because it is based on distrust and the assumption of impending conflict, which is why written contracts between husband and wife, religious superior and subject, make a mockery of the family and religious relationships. These latter can only function on love, faith and hierarchy, no matter how imperfectly. Yet ideals to the contrary, written agreements, rules, and legal sanctions are what the modern world is all about. Very few contractual disputes are settled on the basis of rightness or wrongness. The real question always is: Who will lose more if the dispute goes unsettled? In present day human relations power controls. Who has the power to impose his will on someone else? That power may be a physical or a military fiat, or the tyranny of "majority vote," or the fist of a strategically placed minority power bloc.

Those Who Help Themselves

The Church does not praise this state of affairs but she acknowledges its existence. And in so doing she is willing to call for "power to the poor." This is why she is so favorable to trade unions. Unions cannot create work but they can enforce standards of good employment, especially good wages. And unions probably have done more for the poor than any other organized body. "New" poor may resent the fact that unions do not make it easy to get a membership card, but protecting jobs and protecting old-timers, who once fought rough battles to obtain power, is what trade unionism is all about. Special privilege belongs to those who earn it, not necessarily to the young or to latecomers. Those who remember working conditions less than fifty years ago can assure waiting newcomers how these protections will work to their advantage fifty years hence. Msgr. George G. Higgins is sensitive to the complaints of the "new poor" who in his judgment

> have a perfect right to expect and demand a higher standard of performance from organized labor than from any other institution in American Society with the exception, if you will, of organized religion.[1]

Even so, the Church continues to support these organizations which promote the cause of poor people.

Middle class people, especially those recently up from poverty, tend to forget how much self help in the last generation helped their own have-not parents. Philip Carey, S.J. brings that fact startingly to mind by the recovery of his father's time sheet of one week's work as a trolley motorman, ending March 2, 1913. For the princely sum of $20.99 the senior Carey put in the following hours:

Sunday	10 hrs., 18 mins.
Tuesday	11 hrs.
Wednesday	13 hrs., 30 mins.
Thursday	10 hrs., 25 mins.
Friday	10 hrs., 30 mins.
Saturday	9 hrs., 10 mins.

When the workers organized against those long hours and paltry wages, the company offered to raise pay one cent an hour. The chairman of the railway system gave this solemn warning:

> Don't listen to those union radicals who would wreck your company. We are making a fair offer. If you demand more, you will wreck the railroad. I warn you, if you do you can go back home, get on your knees and confess before God: "It was my greed that destroyed the company."[2]

Even Catholic capitalists seemed to believe that religion really was the opiate of the people. A strike ultimately followed in 1916 but was broken when the company imported outside thugs and strike-breakers. Only World War I brought higher wages, and even then working conditions remained slavish. To earn in 1923 a weekly wage of $69.98 the motorman totalled 97 hours and 15 minutes of "platform time." Fifty years later the unionized motorman receives $249.00 for a forty hour week, medical, pension, holiday and other fringe benefits besides. The old transport worker lived only to work and had little time for his family.

This improvement is more than dollar improvement. Romanticists sometimes refer to the better conditions of the old days when "the dollar bought more." The fact is that the modern worker has a real income four times what his father had. He can buy four times what his father could, even if his father had available the conveniences currently on the market. It is this kind of upgrading which explains why American workers have never become "the proletariat." Goetz Briefs defined the proletariat man as the

> propertyless wage earner who regards himself and his kind as a distinct social class, who lives and forms his ideas in the light of this class consciousness according to class ideals, and who on the basis of this class consciousness rejects the prevailing social and economic order.[3]

The working class in France, Germany and Great Britain have been called the "Lumpenproletariat." Such a designated class status has never been applied to American workers. Even though few Americans own productive property and many more have no desire to be entrepreneurs in their own right, workers in the United States have the security which derives from union contracts and social legislation. The *Communist Manifesto* of Marx and Engels, categorized workers as slaves of the bourgeoisie, law and religion as captives of these same slaveowners. Such assignations never had relevance to the American condition.

This nation early developed a religious and social conscience about the effect of industrialism on working people. Labor had something to do with this. Terence Powderly and his *Knights of Labor* were destined to early deaths. What union could possibly succeed with bankers and brewery workers as members of the same lodge? But Powderly did publicize grievances, the Knights did rally workers and public awareness of social injustice did become a common fact. Business early got the message and developed betterment programs, whose only purpose was to keep unions out.

Samuel Gompers changed all this with his American Federation of Labor. Unions, for a long time thereafter, were organized on a craft basis. Each craft was given exclusive jurisdiction over its own work. Once organized, no one could get a job done without the blessing of the union. This labor power was equal to any power held by those who wanted to build, transport, or sell. As much as any Mogul on Wall Street Gompers believed in laissez faire. Like capitalists, his men would pursue their own interest and in case of conflict were quite ready to take care of themselves. Ever-expanding production and ever-expanding profits made it possible for Gompers to keep asking for more and getting it. Management's vaunted power to run the economy as it pleased was never again to be absolute.

But the Church was important too. James Cardinal Gibbons' successful effort to prevent the condemnation of the *Knights of Labor* by the Holy See gave the Church a pro-labor appearance. Some bishops were concerned about anti-religion in the lodges, but Churchmen correctly decided to bear these difficulties rather than appear to be anti-labor. Especially since it was Catholic workingmen who suffered from poverty and discrimination. Gibbons' action helped prepare the climate within the Church which led Leo XIII in 1890 to promulgate the encyclical *Rerum Novarum,* the "Catholic gospel" which placed the Church four-square behind the cause of workingmen.

However, neither Church nor State rely on trade unionism alone. Social legislation, the educational process itself, cooperative enterprises are the valuable long-range tools for developing economic goals and mutual understanding. Conferences and classes have helped ventilate grievances between classes and develop inter-group accommodation. Laws such as the *Norris-LaGuardia Act,* which limited the power of federal courts to break strikes, or the *Fair Labor Standards Act,* which sets minimum levels of wages and hours, established standards below which social behavior was not permitted to fall. Even the courts, once anti-labor, are now quite even-handed on questions relating to disadvantaged members of society. But the big step forward in the march of social justice was the Wagner Act. When collective bargaining became an essential element of national policy the distribution of the wealth became subject to decision-making by labor, as well as by capital. Dividing the economic pie by mutual consent became commonplace in the United States.

Once workers choose to be unionized, the legal area subject to collective bargaining becomes quite extensive. Not only wages and conditions of employment, but merit increases, incentive pay, rates for new jobs, holidays and vacations, Christmas bonuses, stock bonuses, rental of company-owned houses, the price of meals furnished, discharge, layoffs, retirement, transfers, seniority, downgrading, health and safety, subcontracting became important. The day of the old one-paragraph labor contract went out with the steam engine. Present contracts are a lawyer's paradise.

The type of unions covered by labor contracts also varies. In mass producing industries, thousands of workers without regard to job classification or skill belong to one union—as in automobiles, coal, steel, transportation. This gives union officials a large veto power over what General Motors, U.S. Steel, or Amtrak can do, although the very magnitude of the industries leaves management with almost total control over the labor force. When craft unions are involved, the contracts and management policies are special. The casualness or irregularity of work, or the presence of innumerable small competitive firms, has prompted management to share with the union precious prerogatives. In the building industry, for example, the union has the responsibility for supplying craftsmen, for training apprentices, and for policing wage scales. In the steel industry, the employer guarantees work; not so in construction, where the union by moving men from job to job is the guarantor. (Misuse of this power explains the complaints about union corruption, inflated cost of labor, make-work practices in this industry.)

Regardless of the type, each form of unionism has made its own contribution to the economic betterment of workers. The craft unions certainly made the high hourly wage rate an ingredient of the labor ethos. Philip Murray, dealing with the problem of old steel workers retiring perforce before their time, championed successfully the generous industrial pension, which today is the envy of European visitors to these shores. Walter Reuther's long experience with the vagaries of automobile production is greatly responsible for industrial regulations pertaining to safety and hygiene and equality of opportunity without regard to race or origins. Even in the vast majority of occupations which remain unorganized, these elements of social progress have become part of the employment fabric of the nation.

Not all of these benefits are achieved without a price being paid even by workers themselves. Pension plans make it difficult for men over forty years of age to find work. Equality of wage rates for blacks and whites or for men and women make it difficult for Ford to compete with Volkswagen or Toyota. Ecological concerns, which motivate companies to move out of smog-filled cities, bring strikes in suburbs and on college campuses. One problem solved does not mean an end to problems. The very solution creates difficulties of its own for someone else.

Trade unionism has even improved the lot of workers never contemplated by the original charters. The building service unions which were organized on behalf of doormen and bellhops, now help the dreadfully poor orderlies in nursing homes, whose base pay has recently risen to $155 for a 35 hour week. Tunnel workers and Sand Hogs were among the first to admit blacks. One official looking at the lining plates of the Lincoln Tunnel once asked Father Carey,

> Tell me, now, if you can? What was the color of the arm that tightened this bolt?[4]

The Meat Cutters and Butchers have brought their standards from the slaughter houses of Chicago—once "the hog butcher of the world" to new meat packers in East St. Louis, Cincinnati, Dubuque, and Denver. Retail Clerks, once so full of Irish American Catholic girls, remains quite Catholic in membership, but

Spanish. No occupation has benefited more from a combination of unionization and political action than longshoremen. The waterfront used to be a happy hunting ground for political parties seeking patronage jobs and graft money. Dockmen owed their very lives to politicians and gangsters. Those who did not play the game were unceremoniously murdered. (One dockland emperor boasted thirty submarine or submachine deaths.) Today, registered longshoremen have a title to their job. At one time two-thirds were unemployed three months a year, and the final third were lucky to work four months out of the twelve. Today, dock work is stabilized. One-third of the former labor force, with a guarantee of fifty work weeks a year, handles three times the cargo tonnage. The building-trades are most frequently criticized for not giving jobs to new minorities. Blacks may have little difficulty with organizations such as the Operating Engineers, but soon learn that building crafts are really parochially isolated baronies, each vying with the other to keep their own unemployment at a minimum. Fr. Carey describes the problem:

> The dock builders are from Sweden, carpenters usually Irish, drillers come from Southern Italy, Iron Workers from Halifax when they are not Iroquois Indian, derrickmen, roofers, marblemen, steam fitters have their own special history and make-up. So outsiders, any outsiders, have difficulty, especially when the fight for steady work becomes frantic.[5]

Outsiders, black or white, fail to appreciate the seasonal nature of construction work and the frailty of government building programs. Even so, these restrictive unions are the very associations which through their internationals and federations have probably been one of the most effective lobbyists for civil rights legislation in the country. What is more, the AFL-CIO does pursue these political goals internally. All its constituent unions are required to

> review their contracts and upgrading procedures to conform with equal opportunity standards and to help open opportunities for minority youth and workers.[6]

Evenhanded compliance does not always follow directives, but the civil rights record of labor is hardly inferior to that of other self-interest groups.

Is the Church Pro-Labor?

This is a question frequently asked along with another: Why do so many priests support labor and so few management? John Cronin in his usually balanced manner once expected diocesan social action programs to include close ties to employers.[7] This rarely worked out in practice. First of all, most priests were themselves children of the poor and hardly management-oriented. Secondly, by the disposition of their calling, they were likely to accept as gospel the alleged dictum of the royal St. Louis of France: "Always be on the side of the poor man rather than the rich man until you know the truth." This explains why priests in earlier days rarely crossed a picket line, when men fought to earn more than $25 a week, although it may no longer be the rule in a dispute over a $25,000 annual pay scale.

The more important reason why priests of the past seemed to be pro-labor is that employers did not seem to want priests pricking their consciences. Priest involvement in those days would not likely have been to their advantage. When management holds power it has no need of priests. The few occasions when priests took a pro-management stance, it was for the reason that a particular union cause was wrapped up in violence or left-wing ideology. Generally speaking, management has always been rather suspicious of ecclesial interference in economic affairs. The neutrality of the Church under those circumstances was preferred as the lesser of two evils.

It does not follow, however, that all labor activity has received a certificate of approval from Catholic leadership. The defects of the labor movement may have been frequently glossed over by partisan defenders but never ignored. John Cort describing his work with the *Association of Catholic Trade Unionists* in 1937 and thereafter, observes:

We were worried a good deal about racketeers in some of the

Theodore Lownik Library
Illinois Benedictine College
Lisle, IL 60532

older AFL unions and we tried to help rank and file union members who were inclined to organize themselves, usually unsuccessfully, to cast off the dead hand of corrupt local leaders. One reason for their unsuccess was explained to me when a truck driver made me understand what it feels like to have a gun shoved in your ribs on a dark rainy night.[8]

The United Farm Workers

Nonetheless, the general thrust of the Church was never better exemplified than by the 1973 intervention of the United States Conference of Catholic Bishops on behalf of the *Amalgamated Clothing Workers* and the *United Farm Workers* in their respective disputes with the Farah Manufacturing Company in Texas and the lettuce and grape-growers in California. Here were extraordinary steps by a national body of bishops. Accustomed to the presentation of pertinent moral principles rather than direct action, the bishops in a rare display threw the weight of the Church on the side of the workers. The episcopal assembly decided that without such support, the pants makers and the fruit pickers were not likely to obtain justice or even a union of their own choice. Some Catholics, including some priests on the local scene, were not happy with the decision but the bishops were in agreement that management was interfering in the efforts of depressed minority groups to organize their own union.

Bishops usually acknowledge their incompetence to determine the ingredients of justice in a particular social situation. Other Catholics, sometimes priests, more often Catholic associations, are expected to take up cudgels on behalf of righteous causes. Pastors of all the faithful, such as bishops, cannot choose up sides on issues which have nothing to do with justice, or when the available data seriously divides fair-minded men, all of whom may be bishops' own parishioners. However, elemental matters of basic justice are something else again. Disputes over vacations, pension plans or grievance procedures concern the full life, not justice. But the right to organize, to security against discrimination for labor activity, to wages related to going standards of decency, are areas into which bishops can and should move with assurance. What public opinion will say the day that the official Church comes down equally hard against labor is a matter of some conjecture. Once upon a time, the Church was criticized for supporting unions with a record of violence or Marxism. Nowadays, the contemporary unorganized poor ask: how can the Church support unions whose record of promoting opportunity, equality, shared responsibility, or productivity, has been so bad? Or how can clerics consort with labor leaders who are known among the poor as "porkchoppers?"

Let Us Look At the Record

The sins of organized labor certainly must be acknowledged and confessed. Some of the steam and idealism seem left behind in the graves of pioneers. A labor force of ninety million has no more unionists than thirty years ago, when the force was half this size. New technology has reduced the work force of the unionized industries, while white-collar occupations have prospered without the need of paying union dues. It is also true that prosperous labor leaders are more comfortable in saving the saved. Caring for existing contracts and managing political programs are time-consuming jobs and less expensive than missionary work among the unorganized.

In spite of these shortcomings, it is still fair to say that the greatest friend of the poor is the labor movement. Further, the AFL-CIO is probably the most integrated institution in American society, more integrated than corporations, churches or universities. Minorities, therefore, have most to gain from the collective action of trade unions than from any other group. Currently twelve percent of all union members are black, which is approximately the proportion of blacks in the general population. Even more significant is the new fact that one out of every five apprentices for craft unions are black. The traditional centers of father-son, "our own kind" membership—Irish, Italian, Jewish are opening up to admit blacks, who also have proportionately large numbers in the industrial or public service unions. Derek C. Bok and John T. Dunlop of Harvard University concur:

It is probably correct to say that greater progress has been made in securing equal opportunity in employment than in any other field of American life. Yet, employment is so vital that Negro leaders are understandably impatient with the obstacles still to be overcome. Whether unions can surmount this challenge is a question of profound importance, but the answer remains obscure. With the aid of full employment and more adequate government programs, the problem may eventually be overcome without great turmoil. On the other hand, rejection of Negro claims may lead to attempts to form Black unions in the ghettos and complete alienation from the labor movement. In this respect, the unions are but a larger microcosm of the larger problems confronting all of American Society.[9]

These authors argue further that while critics, especially intellectuals, tend to deprecate labor leaders, business executives at the bargaining table and politicians in city halls make no such mistake.[10]

This does not mean that the introduction of the poor to unionism is an easy task. The experience of the United Farm Workers witnessed the difficulties. California priests first brought the problem of migrant farm workers to the attention of George Meany and Walter Reuther. The AFL-CIO failed to organize farm workers, in part because professional organizers lacked confidence in Chicanos (at least the Chicanos thought so), in part because business unionism did not seem to have much appeal to the Mexican mentality, but more likely because the fluid and intermittent labor supply made organization difficult. Forty years ago, John Steinbeck in the *Grapes of Wrath* and Carey McWilliams in *Factories in the Field* dramatized the scandal of wandering farmers. The canneries ultimately were organized, the truckers were too, but the workers in the field, who stooped low to pick lettuce and the grapes which helped make cannery workers, teamsters and growers prosperous, remained at the mercy of growers. Along came Cesar Chavez who gave his own people a sense of mission, to succeed where others failed.

All initial efforts to organize the unorganized have a built-in tendency to flounder. Failures are repeated before some union makes it. Many idealists promoting a good cause have had their heads bashed in by the enforcers of employers and a rival union, in California frequently by police. Poor people are easily intimidated or bought off. To them half a loaf is better than none, and wives can be eloquent on that point. When the cause seems hopeless, it makes little sense to lay fault at anyone's door. But, when unions succeed it is because of the determination of native leadership, the professionalism of the organizers, and sometimes the help of the Church.

The present generation of the poor, Hispanics and blacks particularly, do not look as readily to the Church for support as their antecedents. In other days the Church always seemed involved even when it was fighting the Molly Maguires, the Wobblies, and the left-wing C.I.O. unions. The secure Church dispensed its favors and its criticism with indiscriminate fervor. In these days, Hispanic alienation may not be the fault of the American Church but a throwback to their native origins and presumptive anti-clericalism. Blacks, as emigres from the Bible Belt, have had little direct contact with the Church, which lately is just another "whitey" institution. Both these groups moved into cities of historic Catholic dominance just about the time Catholic power was disappearing. They might have received better service from the old "powerhouse," but hardly a great deal from a rattled Church, whose priests and religious are leaving, or from a nation whose prevailing mood is disenchantment. Whether judgments on the Church by the new poor are right or wrong, their rejection of the Church will be a severe blow. Even if they assume wrongly that priests and prelates are not interested because the face now is black or has a Spanish tongue, that Church, which has made its kingdoms in the great cities of the world—from Antioch, Corinth, and Rome to New York, Chicago and Los Angeles, will have failed the poor for the first time in generations.

Catholic failure with the poor will be doubly unfortunate because religion and faith are a very big part of their lives. They may go to Church less and have more "religious problems" than the middle class, but their survival as human beings often depends on their faith in the ultimate benevolence of God. Hispanics from Mexico or the Caribbean Islands grew up in a culture where faith in God, in the family, in human dignity was preeminent.[11] They need assurances from men of the Church that their trust in the ultimate victory of faith is well-founded. Throughout their own depressing history in America blacks have turned to the Church as their chief mechanism for survival. At one time the most organized thing in the black's life was done through the Church.[12] If the Church is turned off by aggressive young Hispanics and blacks, it may be that the Churches no longer are seen as instruments of social uplift. Ministers and priests are no longer seen as neighborhood leaders. Activist groups continue to ask for more priests and religious in the ghetto; their presence on the picket line is considered encouraging, and at times has prevented violence in the street and beatings in the jailhouse. But the fact of life is that secular organizations with government money are where the real action takes place.

Yet this is not the entire story. Certainly not the final answer. Long before the civil rights movement, the Catholic Church was very much involved in every ghetto. The ghetto always had a larger proportionate share of religious, usually carefully selected and of superior quality. They were leaders of their people. Even though the Church and the nation were not yet fully awake to the larger goals for racial and ethnic groups, they were respected, even beloved. If the Church is failing today in the ghetto, what can be the reason? Is it because the ghetto religious are not good social crusaders? That cannot really be the reason because they are more articulate defenders of the problems of the poor today than their predecessors. Priests working with earlier ethnics were somewhat mute by comparison. Contemporary priests and nuns—charged up with the value of the secular city and charged out by the Church to engage the world—talk loudly and carry a big stick. Yet they fail to reach the new masses. Why?

It will be temerarious to suggest that there is any one answer to that question. But there is one possible answer which is receiving little hearing. Is it possible that the reason for the contemporary failure of the Church in the ghetto is because ministers there are not seeking the Kingdom of God? In their fulminations against the evils of the present system, in their statements of complaints and objectives, some of them sound little like Jeremias or Christ, and more like Harry Bridges or Saul Alinsky. One sociologist speaks of some who are "converting the gospel into an ideology by seeking justice through a variety of violent efforts."[13] If they are not preaching the Kingdom of God, why should people listen to them at all?

American priests have always been successful with the poor. The sacristy priests were never real persons in this country until recently. Those who are remembered affectionately by the poor of an earlier generation are remembered most for the priestly things they did well. They did them in the sacristy to be sure, but they were just as comfortable blessing, cajoling, or correcting out in full view. As a matter of fact, nineteenth century bishops had a difficult time getting priests to baptize babies in Church, or even to reserve the Blessed Sacrament there. Those priests thought people's homes were good enough. They did a lot of secular things like raising money. But their basic preoccupation was the sacred. They mulled over the bad marriages in the parish and the Mass attendance. Getting children educated in reading so that they could learn the catechism better was second in importance to getting babies baptized and confessions heard. They were also visible priests—in their cassocks or white linen collar—outside the Church on a Sunday morning, in the homes of parishioners during the week. Arbitrating family spats, chasing after delinquent kids, joining people at parties, in the sickroom, at the wake, at the grave came natural to them. They got more kids out of jail than they put in, but were quite adept at scolding because their job was to improve character and temper passion. The priest's week was always full, because every parish seemed to have a disproportionate share of blatherskates, who ducked the priest every chance they got but talked about his great virtues after he died. His work with the young came easier, because he got so many of their fathers to God just in the nick of time. They knew about jobs that no one thought existed, and gave away food like they made it themselves. And when they had to talk to the district leader, the police captain, or the "mayor's man" downtown, they got first-rate treatment because no one could ruin a political reputation better than "father."

Those priests did not solve all their people's problems. Complainers will insist they solved none at all, or made them worse. But they were involved in the lives of their people, not as social workers, not as politicians, but as ministers of a gospel which can lift people above the troubles of a given moment.

The Catholic Church, like the trade union movement itself, became so successful in reaching the poor, channelling them into the middle class, that successive generations of priests, like successive generations of labor leaders, became expert at saving the saved only. Parish priests stopped going out into the highways and byways because people came to them. Seminaries ceased training missionary-minded priests, and bishops became satisfied with a success for which they could take no credit. When new migrants came, who did not know where their father's house was, there was little work for the priests, and it never occurred to many of them to go back out on the streets. One young graduate from Maynooth spent the first five years of his priesthood in an urban ghetto. Within the first year he spoke Spanish with a brogue, and with that one skill and his own industry, he dug 1,500 unchurched Puerto Rican youngsters out of slum pits and gave them religious instruction twice a week. By the second year, he had 1,000 of their parents at Sunday Mass. His technique was not very complicated —visit every Spanish street on evenings when the fathers were home—perhaps five families a night, spend days playing stickball on the street, visiting jails, employment offices, and classrooms. When this particular priest returned to Ireland, the work fell apart. Years later, his successors complained of their difficulties reaching the Puerto Ricans.

It is this neglect of the obvious mission of the Church, and the daily grind it implies, that has prompted some to go the more exciting and the better reported radical route. Against a long Catholic tradition they decided that the way to a Spanish or black heart was through social conflict, only to discover that approval by editorial writers did not necessarily win converts among the masses. Only the hard unnoticed work of personal service in Christ's name—no one else's—would accomplish that. The Lord wants the poor to help themselves for the right reasons too, which is what makes the right kind of priests and religious so important.

NOTES FOR CHAPTER THREE

1 Rev. Msgr. George G. Higgins, St. John's University, May 9, 1974.

2 Cited by Philip J. Carey, S.J., St. John's University, May 11, 1974.

3 Goetz Briefs, *The Proletariat*, (New York: McGraw Hill, 1937), p. 50.

4 Cited by Philip Carey, St. John's University, May 11, 1974.

5 *Ibid.*

6 *Report of the AFL-CIO Executive Council*, Tenth Annual Convention, November, 1973.

7 John Cronin, *Catholic Social Action*, (Milwaukee: Bruce, 1948), p. 63.

8 John Cort, *op. cit.*, pp. 344-345.

9 Derek C. Bok and John T. Dunlop, *Labor and the American Community*, (New York: Simon and Schuster, 1970), pp. 136-137.

10 *Ibid.*, p. 34.

11 See Joseph P. Fitzpatrick "Value, Ethics and Family Life" in Fred Delli Quadri's *Helping the Family in Urban Society*, (New York: Columbia University Press, 1963), p. 78. Also Fitzpatrick's *Puerto Rican Americans: The Meaning of Migration to the Mainland*, (Englewood Cliffs, New Jersey: Prentice Hall, 1971) in which the sixth chapter treats specifically of the Puerto Rican family.

12 Robert B. Hill, *The Strength of Black Families*, (New York: Emerson Hall, 1971) pp. 33-35. See also Martin Luther King, Jr., *Stride Toward Freedom: The Montgomery Story*, (New York: Harper & Row, 1968).

13 Joseph F. Fitzpatrick, S.J., in address entitled "The Poor Family" at St. John's University, May 10, 1974.

CHAPTER FOUR

THE MEANING OF POVERTY FOR THE POOR FAMILY

"How can we do away with the poverty of thousands of families without destroying the deep and significant values which these families so often represent? This is an old and classic theme: the struggle to escape from poverty, disadvantage, destitution, only to realize that the very process which the poor man thought would enrich and ennoble his life, has in fact destroyed it."

REV. JOSEPH P. FITZPATRICK, S.J.
Fordham University

The Jesuit sociologist, whose priestly and professional career has brought him into contact with several generations of multilingual poor, raises a question rarely raised by anyone. What does it profit the poor to be uplifted, if in the bargain they lose something more valuable than money? No one seriously argues in favor of the "tangle of pathology" associated with poverty—bad marriages, bad physical and mental health, bad housing, bad schools, alcoholism, violence, delinquency, crime, drug addiction. Getting the poor larger paychecks and ample cubic air space may leave the silent, hidden, and often irremediable consequences of being poor unattended. But if movement up the economic ladder does not readily remove cultural scars, neither does it save valuable cultural elements, the loss of which involves a high cost of its own. Making it in America can be the unmaking of valuable and ancient cultural strains, the unmaking of a prized sense of family.

Usually, the first thing sacrificed on the altar of progress is the high esteem given to family. The poor look at life differently from the rich. Their family life inculcates a worldview which is not

necessarily inferior. One need not be a scholar to know that for
the poor and for everyone else

> the role of the family in shaping character and ability is so
> pervasive as to be easily overlooked. The family is the basic
> unit of American life; it is the basic socializing unit. By and
> large, adult conduct in societies is learned as a child.[1]

While Moynihan was directing these remarks to the harmful
effects of unstable family life on poor black children, no mention
is made of superior values possessed by the poor, which will be
shuffled off as they ascend the mount of prosperity. Affluent intellectuals are inclined to suggest to the poor virtues which (according to Christopher Jencks they consider "greatly overrated," i.e,,
sexual continence and fidelity,[2] but intellectuals are rarely eloquent on the vices which are handed on to the poor by the dominant culture. It is worthwhile examining the family system of the
poor, if only to discover what they are likely to lose by becoming
middle class.

Every social class has its own way of thinking, its own sense of
the important. Oscar Lewis, after studying the poor of three con-
tinents, immortalized the "culture of poverty" as follows:

> Living in crowded quarters, a lack of privacy, gregariousness,
> a high incidence of alcoholism, frequent resorts to violence in
> the settlement of quarrels, wife beating, early initiation into
> sex, free union or consensual marriages, a relatively high inci-
> dence in the abandonment of mothers and children, a trend
> toward mother-centered families and a much greater knowl-
> edge of maternal relatives, the predominance of the nuclear
> family, a strong disposition of authoritarianism, and a great
> emphasis on family solidarity—an ideal only rarely achieved.[3]

That these characteristics of family life are discoverable in
every ghetto, whether the occupants be Jewish, Irish, Italian,
Puerto Rican or black is a restatement of the obvious. Men in the
ghetto, whose sons are chased by police and priests, may end up

with sons who will be police and priests, but is the Lewis' description of their present family life the whole story? Social commentaries on family life in the ghetto are not always bias-free. The common American assumption is that family life is ideal when few in numbers, free of constraints imposed by older relatives, and when in the family the husband-wife relationship is preeminent, more important than the parent-child relationship. The going "ideal" family unit stands on its own, hardly has any traditions worth transmitting, and is conceived as a mechanism whereby "individuals ideally relate to each other, first of all as human beings, free to express feelings of love and affection, anger or hostility. It is this family which ideally gives emotional security."[4] The presumption is that such family types, frequently found in Crestwood Heights, Toronto, or Shaker Heights, Cleveland, give emotional security. By comparison, traditional families, i.e., those located in working-class neighborhoods, are alleged to shortchange both children and wives because they do not accentuate free expression necessary for sound emotional development.[5]

It is an indisputable fact that most people, given the opportunity, will flee the worst conditions of poverty. The poor man is likely to die ten years too soon. Substandard housing and crowded living are not conducive to longevity. Their sons will never go to college, indeed may be lucky if they learn to read. The odds are two, three, often four times, against them when it comes to losing infant babies, getting sick, being sent to a mental hospital. And growing up in neighborhoods, where the rapes, the murders, crimes are four or five times more general than in other areas, cannot be much fun.[6]

But not all lower class family life is so depressed by living conditions that the members become immoral, uncivilized, promiscuous, and lazy. As a matter of habit, some do. Newcomers, who are psychologically or socially unequipped to cope with the menial dirty jobs and dirty neighborhoods, get their identity by deviant behavior. On the whole, however, lower class family life is quite stable. The people make the most of their opportunities, carry on, or develop, if necessary, a culture which provides them with dignity, approval, and a sense of importance. The family itself is likely to be old fashioned, religious, and tied in with other families, especially relatives. Helping each other is a learned trait vital to survival. The world outside may be unfriendly and hurtful, but not the family. Loud shouting can be heard through airshafts, more drinking goes on than is good for anyone, and the "head" of the household sometimes disappears. But, there is very little chaos. Everyone has assigned or assumed tasks. Obedience is expected and given. Sociologists like to call these families—with their debates, rivalries, and independence—authoritarian. Perhaps because after the debates or when some issue is vital, discipline rules, even if it comes from a slap across the face. Humor and horseplay is common among members who learn to compete, who learn the importance of work, of getting ahead, even if it only means winning the sack-race at the parish outing. Working class people may put a good trade union or civil service job ahead of the college diploma, prefer their own kind before "the brotherhood of man," express themselves strongly rather than with good manners, and prepare their children for all the battles of life, not just one or two.[7] They may be numerous, different and loud, but they are also attached and have a "joie de vivre" of their own.

In recent years, the black community has reacted strongly to repeated denigrations of its family life. White eyes tend to focus on the instability or pathology of family life in the ghetto. Recurring references to the black matriarchate, for example, tend to belie the fact that three quarters of black families are headed by married couples. The strengths of black families, even under the most distressing conditions, are rarely mentioned publicly. Robert Hill lists five most neglected black strengths: (1) the strong kinship bonds which extend beyond the single unit; (2) the flexibility of black parents and youngsters in playing multiple roles important to family maintenance; (3) a rarely acknowledged orientation of poor blacks toward work, (4) and toward achievement, especially in education; (5) their historic religious piety.[8]

Any discussion of the poor family ultimately involves questions of values and meaning. But whose values? Whose meaning? What does it mean to be poor? For a long-arrived WASP perhaps a major catastrophe? For a poor Chicano the opportunity provided by

God to make a better life for his children? Poor families—along with their disasters—have values noticeably in short supply among the affluent. Mutual aid is one such special value. Another is faith in God. The poor share their soybeans and flour, their beds and their children. Family solidarity and family loyalty come natural to the poor, whether Irish, Italian, Jewish or Spanish. The feuds and the bickerings are tossed in to make the game exciting.

Fitzpatrick argues that the central value of new poor, who come from a Catholic culture, is "personal dignity within a context of deep family obligations and relationships."[9] This sense of dignity has earned them the title "proud poor." Michael Novak, a son of a Czechoslovakian immigrant, recently acquired a public reputation simply by defending this ethnic tradition.[10] Poor ethnics, as a group or as individuals, never made it easy in Europe or America. Some hoped to escape pain by denying their backgrounds, by changing their names or religion. But most lived to revel sooner or later, not only in their parents, but in their line and heritage.

Subcultures, once more, are coming into their own, because they are the means by which struggling groups survive in a community whose values and way of life are unfriendly, if not obnoxious. Jews knew this problem in Poland, Catholics, no less than contemporary blacks or Hispanics still know this in WASP America. The melting pot ideal was always a myth invented by Protestants to give immigrants hope and keep them quiet at the same time. The actual fact is that the various subgroups boiled in America without being melted. This durability says something for Jewishness, Irishness and Blackness in a country which theoretically was intended to homogenize everyone into affluent types, even when they were broke.

Until recently, the Catholic subculture prospered. Bishops saw to that. Immigrants were not always law-abiding, and the least law-abiding of any Catholic group were the early Irish. No contemporary racist could speak worse about blacks than what in the nineteenth century was said of the Irish Immigrant. Bishop John Hughes described the Irish debarking from the gangplanks as "the poorest and most wretched population that can be found in the world" and "the scattered debris of the Irish Nation."[11] But practicing or not, Catholics had a special value system, which required protection and promotion. Contrary to the commonly accepted myth that only Protestants worked, Catholics had a work ethic of their own.[12] Over and above making it in the next world, they were out to make it in this world too. As a matter of fact they became masters at balancing earthly priorities, and any study of Catholics in political life will demonstrate that.[13] Praying and hoping for the next life was a proper reward for putting up with husbands, kids, Protestants—and mostly lack of money. They could outtalk most confessors on a given Saturday because they knew what sins were all about—gambling, drink, "keeping company," contraception, abortion, and, though it may come as a surprise, even stealing.

People committed to any vision of life have to make that vision work. They do not always or evenly succeed, and Catholics have volumes of statistics on their lost sheep. But even lost sheep know where the shepherd is leading, which is the genius of a flock with a shepherd. Accommodation is a perfectly acceptable word to poor people. Catholic, Blacks and Jews do it regularly. But assimilation is another thing entirely. Assimilation is translated "abomination," when it means sellout to a society whose values are inferior to the ones he is expected to give up. A dominant secular value may call for a skirt down to the ankle, or no skirt at all, contraception or motherhood, going to war or following peace, work or leisure, babies to till the soil or none to pollute the atmosphere. The religious person picks and chooses his way quite smartly, providing he does not have to do this all by himself.

Joseph Fitzpatrick, after addressing himself to the dignity of man acknowledged in "other cultures," capsulates the present American dilemma—

> The value of our life in the United States is also the value of the individual, but the individual released from the bonds and ties of family, the individual in terms of opportunity for purely individual achievement.[14]

American culture prides itself on the opportunities it provides for self-development and self-aggrandizement. Certainly, within limits, these are not unimportant values. But they are individualistic values—the ego-seeking of persons, not the strength of families. By this standard, a family is to be judged on the declared satisfactions or dissatisfactions of each of its members, not on the total family accomplishment. If some people make it, it makes little difference if the family does not make it. If the family does not make it, likely it is that many of its members will make it, especially if one of them acquires a lot of money.

For ethnic families, the central concern is "getting along" and "the children." For the dominant American family-type, the chief goal is "getting ahead," enjoying the American way of life. *Family One* suffers the strain of inadequate income for the basics of life, money for the doctor or for shoes. On the other hand, mother in this family is always home and father presides at the evening meal, where the children learn some of life's ABC's. *Family Two* has its own money burdens. Son Johnny cannot get a car or take a trip to Europe. Father holds two jobs, and sends mother out to work, too. Family decisions do not concern the family as such. No one is inclined to compare the value of accumulated goods and improved social status with the value of another brother or sister. Only much later in life is thought given to the meaning of life without close family ties.

The confrontation between old Catholic-Jewish family systems with Protestant culture has been going on for some time. The secular city says the family is important if it encourages or guarantees personal fulfillment. For the traditionally-religious, family is more than the pairing of man and woman for purposes which the couple decides are gratifying. The family is a network of other families and other cultures. It reaches into the past, covers more than one nuclear unit, and transmits to future generations a particular value system, usually of religious origin. On the other hand, sociologists today are willing to admit that the isolated nuclear family may be a myth or else how can one explain so many crowded bridges on Mother's Day?[15]

Italians may not achieve success like othre ethnic groups, whose values more closely match that of the dominant society, e.g., Jewish,[16] but among both Jews and Italians there is an undeniable network of functioning families. Individualists, be they artists, poets, revolutionaries pay a high price in social terms for individuality. Preordained personal fulfillment is his psychic must, even if it never satisfies. But for most people, psychic fulfillment is a treacherous guessing game. Only after all options have been exercised do most people know they have it or not. But those rooted in a family, tied to a world larger than itself, learn to be realistic about personal fulfillment. They deal not in fantasy about excitement but in terms of a job which must get done.

Some sociologists have given up on the possibility of a family having formative power in modern society. Their expectation is that family strength will derive from couple-initiative, from couples integrating without extrinsic support the values and satisfactions which give their union stability. It is being said that social supports for the family no longer exist and "strong family life will have to come through education, social influence, public opinion and the deepening of religious faith."[17] John L. Thomas, S.J., once an outstanding defender of mechanisms necessary to protect people's values against dominant culture patterns,[18] now argues that even Catholic leaders must accept the radical implications of the "socio-cultural changes reshaping modern conceptions of sex."[19] In simple terms he means that once the Joneses dominate, the D'Agostinos and Rodriguezes must fall in line. Social practice becomes a moral imperative. Theologian Charles Curran, by insisting that the Church must come to realistic terms with the fact that the majority of Americans, including Catholics, favor divorce, says the same thing.[20]

Contrariwise, secular sociologists have begun to question the validity of too-ready concessions to the dominant culture. Intellectuals have too readily identified middle-class family life with the institutionalization of sexual puritanism, without questioning its basic Protestant social ethic. But Miller and Reismann ask some pointed questions:

> Do we attempt to make the middle-class style of life a model for all to follow? Or do we adopt a rigid cultural relativity

position that the lower class has a right to its way of life regardless of the social effects? Or do we attempt to develop what appears to be the most positive elements, from the viewpoint of society and the individuals involved, of the life styles closest to them?[21]

What are the "positive values" of lower and working class families worth sheltering, worth transmitting? Different social classes give different answers, but the differences are often mistakenly converted into rigid stereotypes. American parents, for example, are reported as more likely than Italian parents to value personal happiness. Italian parents are reported as more likely to stress obedience, Americans to be child-centered, Italians as adult-centered.[22] In the real world parental syndromes are strikingly similar, differing only in priorities made by circumstance. The poor are quite realistic about what is necessary to survive, about what is beyond their reach. Princes search for paupers more commonly than the other way round. This same realism colors the education of offspring by the poor. Elemental concepts likely to be passed in the ghetto to the next generation include the following:

1. Marriage is a work to be done, not necessarily a psychic delight. Religious Catholics call marriage a vocation from God himself. This slant on marriage is an important departure from the aspirations of college-educated Americans. The stress is on the trust, the responsibility associated with running a family. Self is important—particularly the status of "mom" and "dad,"—but not so important as "the other," whether spouse or children.

2. Togetherness is good—but it is everybody's togetherness, not just husband and wife. Ethnic spouses have more mutuality than sociologists can measure, but lack of togetherness does not prevent either from acting out the necessary rules for family maintenance.

3. Children are important—the essential *finis operis* of marriage. Although extreme efforts are made to demolish large families, the poor are never anti-child. Taking care of babies is part of the family sport.

4. Religion is important. Poor people are likely to see God's

design in little things. Marriage is not the grim business frequently written up in a psychiatrist's notebook. Being poor does not crush them. Even sickness seems to augment love and attachment. The prayer of the poor housewife is a simple one: "Since I have no time to be a saint by storming heaven's gates, make me a saint by washing up the plates."

5. The family is a central value, so are family ties. Life does not rest on frail human emotions alone but on bonds—ties to each other, ties to God, if need be, but ties that tend to make relationships permanent.[23]

These family values of the working class and the poor are not mere special cultural defenses against the harshness of life. They are part of the Christian patrimony. From the beginning the Church had a difficult time obtaining general acquiescence of the masses to the ideals of Christian marriage. The early apostles and their immediate successors were a new moral force within the Roman Empire, but even they had difficulty. The ascetic lives of the earlier followers of Christ were impressive, but in Paul's time railings against the lasciviousness, fornication, adultery, and homosexuality of Christians began to appear. Persistently the Church did its utmost to preserve the sanctity of marriage and the basic role of the family—even against its own membership. Though higher and lower levels of observance always existed—some able and willing to sacrifice more for the holier life—the Church never relented on the essential values, many of which are typified in the working class family. Certainly, the core place of the family in the Church—its purposes, its ties, its sacredness—is probably still central to Catholicism, and probably an inhibiting factor in the unrestricted pursuit of worldly success by Catholics.

But a new dawn may be breaking on the Church. The family is now defined without reference to children at all. Alvin Toffler provides the warning, when he predicts that "the fractured family" will take the place of that which for a long time followed "the orthodox format." Large numbers will remain traditional, but in the end innovative minorities—with their childless marriages, professional parenthood, post-retirement child rearing, corporate families, communes, geriatric group marriages, homosexual family units, polygamy—allegedly will determine the family form of the future. What Toffler understands as an orthodox family indicates how far the working-class family is behind the times:

> The orthodox format presupposes that two young people will "find" one another and marry. It presupposes that the two will fulfill certain psychological needs in one another, that the two personalities will develop over the years, more or less in tandem, so that they continue to fulfill each other's needs. It further presupposes that this process will last 'until death do us part.' These expectations are built deeply into our culture. It is no longer respectable as it once was to marry for anything but love. Love has changed from a peripheral concern of the family into its primary justification. Indeed, the pursuit of love through family life has become, for many, the very purpose of life itself.[24]

Not only are children incidental to such love (children can be bred and breaded in other ways) but they serve the couple's love, not the other way round. Conjugal love becomes not a force fashioning new lives, but an end in itself. Kinship ties or religious meanings are available options but hardly necessary, and frequently troublesome, to adventures in the game of that psychic fulfillment called marriage. While Toffler's *affective* marriage is assuredly the preferred current type, by any Catholic standard it is hardly an orthodox family.

Yet, the family which enhances a couple's delight is free of the burdens which wear poor people down, especially in the ghetto, where people's only delight may be the television set. The process by which children of the poor are made ashamed of what their parents stand for comes easy in this country. One Italo-American public school teacher wrote an entire book on the debriefing given such children by American educators.[25] It is not so easy to trace the steps by which values inherent in the traditional family and the Church have been sucked out of modern marriage leaving the shell frailly intact. No one thing did it. Ideas and inventions over several centuries changed the family from the "Little Church" of St. John Chrysostom to the playground favored by contemporary authors. Martin Luther started it all by denying there was anything particularly holy about marriage. Two in one flesh was just another part of this world's life, of no great concern to the Church. John Calvin did not intend the next development, but his stress on predestination and "inner-worldly asceticism" made accumulation of riches a sign of God's approval. After a bumpy start, capitalism made life easier, and separated the working husband from his family. Eventually, babies became, not blessings, but more mouths to feed. It was not long before fool-proof contraceptives made babies no longer a great problem for married or single. Even in failure, a skilled abortionist is now available in the wings of life. Sigmund Freud's disciples made the world orgasm-happy. Words like "self-fulfillment," "self-actualization," "self-satisfaction" became jargon for the young. Depressed Protestant theologians decided that God was not God, but man himself moving to Godhood. The Bible and the Church which once were helpful in pointing the way to man, now are in the way of those trying to construct the new man-made Garden of Eden.[26] The new theology of hope, along with increasing access to money and leisure, gives promise to mankind of that beatific state earlier lost by Adam.

The only trouble for Catholics is that the Church no more approves Secular Humanism than she approved Gnosticism, Manicheism, Albigensianism, or Jansenism. Many of her people will, including the children of the poor. Radical theologians of major and minor stature[27] hope that Christian freedom to experiment with sex, marriage, and family life will no longer be limited even by the most profound or hallowed scriptural or traditional insights. The secularization of family life is likely to continue until it exhausts itself in the social vices now everywhere beginning to appear. The Church, however, continues to deny the attribution "Christian" to this experimentation.

In such circumstances what is possible to the Church? Nothing less than preaching and teaching effectively its own doctrines to its own people, to develop within the Church and, if possible, within society, the supports necessary to keep its own special view of marriage alive. This is not a new difficulty. The Church every day faces the cultures of Communist or Islamic nations, or primitive cultures of Africa or South America, with no less tension than in more pleasure-seeking America. Differences everywhere exist whereby the roles of husband and wife, the relationships of parents and children, and of families among themselves are acted out in the concrete. These cultural fences may be high or low, may remain standing or may fall, but the job of the Church remains to have its own people respect, if they do not always honor, marriage of man to woman, for life, in which children have a revered place and wherein the end of striving—the purpose of behavior in-between—is the Kingdom of God.

Following World War II, the Church did rise to the challenge of educating children of the pre-War poor to the noble idealism of Catholic family life. The *Cana Conference Movement,* which was the brainchild of Chicago priests, turned out to be one of the most dynamic apostolic efforts of the Church in the United States. Hardly a diocese in the country lacked parish cells of couples and priests dedicated to making their marriages truly Catholic. The tune of the *Cana Manifesto* of 1949 is in sharp contrast to the depressing this-worldly quality of so much contemporary writing on family life.

— Because we—husbands and wives—are called to love one another as Christ loves and is loved by the Church;

— Because the life of that Church, His Mystical Body, is nourished by the welfare, the holiness of our marriages;

— Because our children, His tenderest branches, are nourished likewise by that holiness;

— *WE SEEK THE HELP,* pledged at the Marriage Feast of Cana and our own nuptials—

— That our sorrows, our hardships, our drudgery, our countless daily irritations may be transformed into a loving gift to each other and to God,

— That our joys may be offered joyously,

— That our marriages may become a prayer, an oblation, a giving of the one thing which is ours to give—our life together as husband and wife, mother and father.

— And that the splendor of Christ's love mirrored in us may
draw others to their true life in Him.[28]

At one point at least 500,000 Catholic couples and 2,000 priests
spread across an entire continent were organized into Cana Clubs,
Christian Family Movement cells, Holy Family Guilds, Cana
Houses for one purpose—to promote and advance the ideals of
Catholic family life. They worked. They had influence on parish
life, on high schools and courses. They wrote books and articles,
talked on radio and television, held conventions, went on retreat
together, grew holy together, loved their priests and bishops.

There was nothing like it for its dynamism, idealism, and per-
vasive influence, in the recent history of the Catholic Church. For
twenty years the Cana Movement dominated Catholic apostolic
works. The pioneer couples were children of those who suffered
through the depression, educated mostly in Catholic schools, themselves the parents of large families, moving to the suburbs, suc-
cesses in the world as they were in the Church. Shortly before
Vatican II, Cana and CFM groups began to turn their attention
to the Spanish population, which by 1960 had become a significant
though not overwhelming segment of the large dioceses.

But then all hell broke loose in the Church. The discovery that
certain hormones ingested by women stifled ovulation raised
proper questions about the possibility that such "pills" might not
come under the Catholic anti-contraceptive ban. Since they were
chemical, not mechanical, and since all kinds of chemicals could
be taken for all sorts of reasons, the possibility of some development on this subject seemed real. The subsequent inundation of
the Church by pro-contraceptive argumentation need not concern
us here, save to say that a correct discussion led to a revolution.
But the very process of fighting over birth control halted the
Catholic family life apostolates in their tracks. Some of them became energetic allies of the Planned Parenthood Federations.

The lesson to be restated here is that any family life gospel,
which seeks to keep alive those values still associated with the
families of the poor and the working class requires from the
Church something like a resurrected Cana Movement. Unlike

some post-Vatican II efforts to reach married couples by sensitivity
sessions (which really result in self-realization, not necessarily in
a new Christian mode), the Cana Movement was an effort to put
on to people that mind which, Paul said, was in "Christ Jesus our
Lord." It had its emotional gratifications, but the primary thrust
was intellectual, doctrinal, support, piety and Catholic identity.

Poor families moving into new generations need this very thing
if they are to keep what the Church deeply feels are essential
familial values for those who profess the Catholic faith. The Catholic middle class may be in greater need of this resurgence. But
the second time around, bishops must make a better judgment
about what supporting institutions best enforce core Catholicism.
They exercised good judgment when they established Catholic
schools. They made a mistake about the Cana Movement. Cynics,
even those with a sense of humor, used to call the approval of the
bishop the kiss of death. Unquestionably there are evidences of
truth in such a blanket assertion. But worth stating with stronger
force is the principle that nothing perdures in the Church unless
it is locked into bishops. As strong as the Cana Movement became
by 1963, its young promoters had to fight their way into the
National Catholic Welfare Conference, the house arm of the
bishops. Diocese by diocese Cana remained approved or tolerated,
growing in influence, without bishops ever sensing the importance
of what was going on ten blocks from the Cathedral. Only after
1965, when the movement began to crumble, did it become clear
that nothing was left in the Church supportive of Catholic
family life at a time of great confusion.

The poor will carry on old traditions for awhile, ones which
they inherited thoughtlessly from their Catholic forebearers. But
alone they too will pass. The Catholic Church, no one else, can
preserve the Christian family as we know it for its own people,
including the poor. John Rock wrote a book in 1963 which sounded
a call to the troops that *The Time Has Come* for contraception.
That time by all accounts is here. But the time may have come
again for the Church to march once more out into the market-
places of the great cities and say again what a Peter said once:

"Men of America, and all of you who dwell in New York, Chicago, and points West, let this be known to you, and give ear to my words."[29]

NOTES FOR CHAPTER FOUR

1 Daniel P. Moynihan and Paul Barton, *The Negro Family: The Case For Action*, (Office of Policy Planning and Research, U.S. Department of Labor, Washington, D.C., Superintendent of Documents, March, 1965), p. 5.

2 Christopher Jencks, *The Moynihan Report*, reviewed in the *New York Review of Books*, October, 1965 p. 218. For an evaluation of this approach to Negro Poverty see Lee Rainwater and William L. Yancey, *The Moynihan Report and the Politics of Controversy*, (Cambridge, Mass.: M.I.T. Press, 1967).

3 Oscar Lewis, *The Children of Sanchez*, (New York: Random House, 1961), p. 26.

4 J. R. Seeley, R. A. Sim and E. W. Looskey, *Crestwood Heights*, (New York: Basic Books, 1956), p. 162. This was a study of a heavily Jewish group in Toronto.

5 Herbert Gans, *The Urban Villages*, (New York: Free Press, 1962), pp. 45-57.

6 See *Social Indicators*, 1973 passim.

7 For a good description of this kind of family see S. M. Miller and Frank Riessman, "The Working Class Subculture: A New View," *Social Forces*, vol. 9, (Summer, 1961), pp. 86-97.

8 Robert B. Hill, *The Strength of Black Families*, (New York: Emerson Hall, 1971). Also, John H. Scanzoni, *The Black Family in Modern Society*, (Boston: Allyn & Bacon, 1971), shatters many commonly held beliefs about urban black family life.

9 Joseph P. Fitzpatrick, "Values, Ethics and Family Life" in Fred Delliquadri, *Helping The Family in Urban Society*, (New York: Columbia University, 1963), ch. 6.

10 Michael Novak, *The Rise of the Unmeltable Ethnics' Politics and Culture in the Seventies*, (New York: Macmillan, 1972).

11 A letter of John Hughes to the Society of the "Propagation of the Faith" (Paris) dated June 26, 1849, and quoted from the archives of the University of Notre Dame in Jay P. Dolan's *Urban Catholicism: New York City 1815-1865* (Unpublished Doctoral Dissertation, University of Chicago, 1970, p. 61.) Emmet Larkin ("The Devotional Revolution in Ireland 1850-1875," *American Historical Review*, June, 1972, p. 651) says: "Most of the

two million Irish who emigrated between 1847 and 1860 were part of the pre-famine generation of non-Catholics, if indeed they were Catholics at all."

12 Andrew Greeley, "The Protestant Ethic: Time for a Moratorium," *Sociological Analysis,* Vol. 25 (Spring, 1964), pp. 20-33.

13 A sample list of books dealing with Catholics in political life would include the following:

See Farley, James Aloysius, *Behind the Ballots; The Personal History of a Politician,* New York: Harcourt, Brace & Co., 1938; Farley, James Aloysius, *Jim Farley's Story,* New York: Whittlesey House, 1948; McKean, Dayton David, *The Boss, The Hague Machine in Action,* Boston: Houghton Mifflin Co., 1940; Moscow, Warren, *The Last of The Big-Time Bosses; The Life and Times of Carmine De Sapio and the Rise and Fall of Tammany Hall,* New York: Stein & Day, 1971; White, Theodore Harold, *The Making of the President* 1960, New York: Atheneum Publishers, 1961; Huthmacher, J. Joseph, *Senator Robert F. Wagner and the Rise of Urban Liberalism,* New York: Atheneum, 1968; Walsh, Thomas James, *Tom Walsh in Dakota Territory,* Urbana, University of Illinois Press, 1966; O'Keane, Josephine, *Thomas J. Walsh, A Senator From Montana,* Francetown, N.H.M. Jones Co., 1955; Mathewson, J., *Up Against Daley,* La Salle, Illinois: Open Court, 1974.

14 Rev. Joseph Fitzpatrick, St. John's University Symposium, May 10, 1974.

15 Eugene Litwak, "Occupational Mobility and Extended Family Cohesion," *American Sociological Review,* 25 February, 1960, pp. 9-21, Fred L. Studtbeck, "Family Interaction, Values and Achievement" in David C. McClelland et. al., *Talent and Society,* (Princeton, New Jersey: Van Nostrand, 1958), pp. 135-195.

16 Catholic political effort in recent years has been less than successful. See George A. Kelly, *Government Aid to Non-Public Schools: Yes or No?* (New York: St. John's University, 1972).

17 Joseph P. Fitzpatrick, *op. cit.,* p. 78.

18 John L. Thomas, S.J., *The American Catholic Family,* (Englewood Cliffs, New Jersey: Prentice-Hall, 1956).

19 John L. Thomas, S.J., "Family, Sex and Marriage in a Contraceptive Culture," *Theological Studies,* vol. 35, no. 1, March 1974, p. 146.

20 See *National Catholic Reporter,* vol. 10, no. 45, October 18, 1974, pp. 1, 18; 7, 14.

21 S. M. Miller and Frank Riesmann, *op. cit.,* p. 97.

22 Leonard I. Pearlin and Melvin Kohn, "Parental Values," *American Sociological Review,* v. 1. 31 (August, 1966), pp. 367-370.

23 For a Catholic view of marriage and family life see George A. Kelly, *The Catholic Marriage Manual,* (New York: Random House, 1958), pp. 3-18.

24 Alvin Toffler, *Future Shock,* (New York: Bantam Books, 1974), p. 249.

25 Leonard Covello, *The Heart is the Teacher,* (New York: McGraw-

Hill, 1958).

26 For a good description of how these ideas influenced history see John A. Hardon, *Christianity in The Twentieth Century*, (Garden City, New York: Doubleday & Company, 1971), p. 366ff.

27 A minor work but nonetheless a graphic presentation of the ultimate meaning of sexuality for the liberated Catholic is Michael F. Valente's *Sex: The Radical View of a Catholic Theologian*, (New York: Bruce, 1970). He is realistic enough, though disappointed, to sense that "the reactionary character of *Humanae Vitae* and the statements of some of the national hierarchies make one wonder how much, if at all, official Church teaching has changed." p. 36.

28 Cited in *The Cana Conference Proceedings—1950* (21 West Superior Street, Chicago, Illinois).

29 Ac 2, 14.

CHAPTER FIVE

DEVELOPING THE POOR COMMUNITY

Stupid America, see that Chicano
See that Chicano with the big knife in his steady hand
He doesn't want to knife you
He wants to sit on a bench and carve Christ figures
But you won't let him.

Stupid America,
Hear that Chicano shouting curses on the street.
He is a poet without paper and pencil,
And since he can not write, he will explode.

Stupid America,
Remember that Chicano flunking Math and English.
He is the Picasso of your Western states,
But he will die with one thousand masterpieces
Hanging only from his mind.

A Chicano Song

Ben Franklin once had the bright idea that one way to do good for the poor was to "drive them out of it." Two centuries later Bob Moses decided the answer to the poor man's prayer was a bulldozer. Neither plan worked. Bullying or bulldozing really does nothing for poverty and makes the poor more miserable. In fact, new housing of the high rise variety usually destroys one of the few consolations the poor in the ghetto have—their sense of togetherness. Improved sanitary conditions may mark the end of community. Upper-class suburbia spends a fortune on professional talent artificially to develop what comes natural to a tenement street. In the slums of the West End of Boston, where racial disturbance reached violent proportions last year, the Italian-Americans living there were described as *urban villagers,* because their deeply entrenched relationships were uncharacteristic of megalopolis.[1]

In their own good time, the poor leave their ghetto, usually by the second or third generation. But while there, the "we-ness" is as important as the bread, something manicured social planners count for little in comparison with the superior value of their "grand plan." Natural areas of companionship may be dirtier, but they are more friendly too, which also explains why middle class ethnics—Jews, Italians, Irish, Poles—have begun to fight with fierceness the attempt by government to break up their neighborhoods, to favor at their expense some other ethnic or radical group.

The "guardian society" of Alexander de Tocqueville may have arrived sooner than we think. At least bureaucracy has, and also the detested bureaucrats without which business, politics, collective bargaining, even religion would come to a halt. The newer social directory, OEO, HUD, VISTA, SNICK, perhaps even a SNEE, are only the recently baptized progeny of NRA, AAA, NYA, not forty years old. What began in 1933 as a simple effort to eliminate "the fear of fear" has become a total war—from Food Stamps, Head Start and National Health Insurance to Talent Search, Upward Bound, and Vista. John Kennedy at his inauguration in 1960 seemed to reflect the determination of the nation: "If a free society cannot help the many who are poor, it cannot save the few who are rich." The only trouble with the idea is that the poor being uplifted are many miles and many social levels away, managed by people whose brain is stored in the computer center. Whatever the justification, and however understandable, this is the essential fact of contemporary life.

Government has become a special kind of bureaucracy. It is not merely that life in society and relationships have been complicated by the amount of technical knowledge required to get something done. The disbursement of unimaginable amounts of public money by potential thieves to potential thieves calls for strict regulations and tiers of supervision. The web of control is so intricate that catching and jailing real live culprits takes years, and

often costs many times the amount diverted to private use. Is it
any wonder, therefore, that standards are enforced without regard
to anyone's personal feeling? The rational answer to the "spoils
system" has turned into a monster. Public benefits are not dispensed by understanding a fellow man's need but by a book intended to guarantee objective fairness. A system invented to prevent favoritism to friend or relative frequently appears unfriendly
and irrelevant to real need. The school is not interested in the
brilliance of the child, but in the month he was born. Social Security does not care about the sick husband, but does he qualify
under existing guidelines?

Management procedures flowing from the so-called ethos of
objectivity possess one other feature which makes them unpalat-
able. Only a few people, sometimes in a polychromed back room,
make the hard and fast rules by which everyone else must live.
Things are no different whether the rule makers are Democrats
or Republicans. "Outs" behave no differently when they become
the rascals who invent restrictions of their own to work to the
advantage of their friends. Daniel Bell remarks the irony of the
fact

> ... that in the school system Jews "used" the merit system to
> dispossess the Catholics who had risen through patronage, but
> that the merit system was now a means of keeping out Blacks
> from high place in the system.[2]

Functionaries, therefore, American Democrats, Russian Socialists,
Curial Cardinals, not the popular president or saintly pope, are
"the power elite." They can sabotage policy-makers any time they
declare some policy to be irrational, i.e., opposed to their way of
thinking.

Obviously they get things done. Without computers, for example, no one would really know how poor the poor are or how many
they number. Without research buildings inventing new techniques of production, how would new opportunities of employment
be conceptualized? Social security payments, unemployment or
AID checks reach their destination faster and more accurately and
are used more economically in the computer-priced supermarkets

than ever was possible in the corner grocery store of the hand-craft era.

Yet somehow the poor, along with the middles, must learn how to deal with the system when it breaks down. The dysfunctions of bureaucracy are always massive. The Bureau which claims 200 percent more production this year than last never makes a small mistake. When one aged Mary Doe does not receive her check, chances are 999 more did not either. The sick sixty-four year olds, who will never make sixty-five, only make government rich if they do not have help in realizing some return on four score years in the social security system. The thousands of brilliant but under-age first grade candidates need alternatives to lying around another year viewing Sesame Street, which may save the system but destroy them.

Managers of bureaucracies frequently forget why their bureau was established in the first place. No one can argue against their dedication and hard work. But the older the Bureau, the more rigid the rules, and the fewer the people with power to deviate or make exceptions. As the laws governing education become more cumbersome, schools become precise about the disbursal of free lunches and the credentials of visiting dentists, and sometimes fail to teach children to read. Religious activists become so involved in picket lines and marches that they fail to remember their basic calling. One World War II naval chaplain rose the morning of the invasion of Africa, November, 1942 to shower, shave, bathe himself in Old Spice, deck himself out in a spotless white uniform, spend the day skirting cannon fire and administering the last rites to bloody sailors, only to collapse that night exhausted realizing for the first time that not once during that day had he paused to say a prayer in his own name or on his own behalf.

Formalized and seemingly irresistible routines prompt some people to throw up their hands or perhaps a bomb or two. But the smart people are those who know how to make bureaus sensitive to their causes.

In the political arena these men of influence are called "lobby-ists." These are the men who stand in a gallery—or a porch—or, if you will, in a lobby—and direct attention to situations politicians would prefer to forget. Lobbyists point the finger and, if necessary, roll up the sleeve. They traffic in pressure. They press a cause and sometimes a button, otherwise spelled "vote." The AFL-CIO's Congress of Political Education (COPE) is pretty good at this, but so is the American Medical Association, the Chamber of Commerce, the Friends of Earth, the National Education Association, NAACP, the American Conservative Union, the American Jewish Committee. Bureaucrats and elected officials live in eternal terror of the powerful lobbyists, who may just see that they get run out of office, if the official does not behave. Lobbyists exist to get laws and regulations drawn up in their favor, or at least less harmful to their cause. Vested interests of all kinds scrutinize with partisan care every piece of legislation affecting them. And officials soon learn that rewards are given to good boys. Those who consistently ignore advice are in trouble. The name of the game, for all sides of the political spectrum, is reward and punishment, a game that the Catholic Church in recent years plays badly.

Very few citizens have the least idea of how a word like "may," "ought," "should," "must" alters a suggested legal or social practice. "Loopholes" do not walk into agencies or courtrooms all by themselves. Exclusion or inclusion under the law, the timing of its effective date, the base year for determining wage or price improvements, the qualifications for coverage, make the difference between effective or ineffective legislation. A specific phrase may confer a benefit. Another may deny it. The *National Education Association* and the *American Jewish Congress* have spent half a lifetime denying public assistance to children attending non-public schools. When in 1964 Lyndon B. Johnson rescued the federal-aid-to-education bill from oblivion by supporting aid to the disadvantaged children of the country, regardless of the school they attended, these organizations, abetted by the *National Council of Churches,* worked feverishly to see that the HEW regulations required remedial reading, remedial math or guidance services be available to non-public school children only in a public school, even if that was miles away and could only be provided after the normal six hour school day was over. That the effort did not entirely succeed is a tribute to the vigilance of two good lobbyists, Hugh L. Carey and Eugene P. Molloy.[3] Had the enemies of religious schools won that battle, poor children in Catholic, Jewish and Lutheran schools would have been denied the benefits of the *Elementary and Secondary Education Act,* even though their participation was precisely why the Johnson Administration succeeded in passing the first federal education law in history!

To many the task of sensitizing bureaucracy seems somewhat hopeless. If a combination of high political-ecclesiastical muscle is required to obtain crumbs from the table of an unfriendly establishment, what are the chances of people who lack capacity for that determination and the means of admission to the halls of influence? Only last year Hugh Carey confessed that the *Job 70 Program,* which was expected to help the third poorest segment of New York City, Jews in Borough Park, Brooklyn, was unable to find the money which had been appropriated for that particular purpose.

In spite of all these difficulties, political pressure—rewarding friends and punishing enemies—is precisely what the democratic process is all about. The question is, however: Who is going to exercise such pressure on behalf of the poor? Who will rate bureaucrats and legislators for doing nothing on behalf of the poor? Those who cover the Washington scene take care of the large vested interests, but who takes care of Newburgh, West Boston, Aurora, or Calexico? Usually no one. It is precisely this vacuum that the churches can fill, providing they fill it well. They can be partisans of the poor, without necessarily being blind leaders of the blind. Presumptively, churches are seekers after justice and above cheap politics. They are as entitled as anyone else to assign "contracts" to public officials. Getting the street cleaned or rolling back rents are small contracts, but reallocating millions of education dollars, building a public office building here rather than there, are big league issues. Reports of contracts completed or ignored constantly turn up on the front pages of the *New York Times* and the *Washington Post.* Publicity, like light, illumines goodness and badness.

But to play this game, which is often ugly, calls for involved people who care. Old ethnic communities, even some of the new, find it easier to withdraw into a shell, to permit decay rather than be bruised by the vulgarities of the contemporary democratic process, which is often dominated by mini-mobs. Here is where the Church comes into the picture. Clergy, if they have sense, character and pray, are natural leaders of community causes. In another generation the Vereins, the Ancient Order of Hibernians, the Mafia took care of things. People at the top of the political machinery had some kinship with those at the bottom. Or they developed kinship to get votes. But now some new support system is needed because things are not right.

The Church must sell a fact of life which she knows, better than anyone else, to be true: government cannot really run things as well as local communities. Social security payments are better distributed by computer, but never does service to human beings and technical efficiency go hand in hand. Any poor person in his right mind prefers St. Clare's Hospital to the more richly endowed and staffed, but publicly owned, Bellevue Hospital. But since not all the poor can get into a small St. Clare's, most end up in the very large Bellevue. But the Church, as one of society's largest institutions, has influence possessed by the few, if the Church dares exercise it. Better than most, Church leaders live with the ghetto poor who are killing themselves striving for the next step on the ladder, by hook or by crook. The Church has to become the moral spokesman of the poor. Who else? Not the investor, not the revolutionary, each of whom lives in his own dream world. Bernadette Devlin, the erratic defender of Irish causes, once advised do-gooding itinerant Americans: "Don't have a glorious parade or wave a banner or send a few bucks and think you are going to help the people of Northern Ireland. Send us the right people." Perhaps what she had in mind was the right kind of bomb-throwers. But in the right context she was correct. The right people always solve critical difficulties. What the poor need are right people speaking in their name and acting on their behalf.

When the Church dares, it does many useful things—builds housing for the elderly, conducts credit unions in low income neighborhoods, or provides remedial education for inadequately trained adults. No privately owned institution in the world—whose space alone represents millions of dollars of Catholic money and thousands of lives—can afford to be more daring. To use these properties and people in support of sound community causes, which involve other than committed Catholics, may represent a departure from customary practice, but enlivens the Church, even if all members do not agree. Once upon a time unions were formed in secret, strikers were fed, the political assemblied were financed, leaders were trained in the front and back yards of the Church. If it was right and proper to open a clinic in the mountainside of Lima, Peru or a school in Trichinopolis, India, encouraging people to fight for their rights is also a laudable work by the Church on West Street, U.S.A.

Once upon a time Catholics identified their residence by name of parish, not by street number. Why? Because the Church was the community, even for Catholics who made Mass occasionally. The parish priests were involved in their human situations and at times people's spokesmen. These social bonds humanized an entire tenement area, and, when the priests were about their real business, affected the soul-life too. People rally round leaders, when those leaders make the people's needs their own. Properly harnessed this togetherness means political power. Politicians pay attention to the churches and synagogues which have great influence on votes. The more recent political troubles of churches are traceable to their failure to remain vital community organizations. Daniel Patrick Moynihan succinctly stated the condition of Catholic power: "They were a minority and had better get used to behaving as such."[4]

Indeed, Catholics became a minor power, even while their numbers were still major. While remaining relatively efficient mechanisms for distributing goods—schooling, sacraments, entertainment, parishes no longer were the center of group-life in the community. In many cities of the United States after World War I, clergy tended to become sacristy priests. They took good care of the people who came to them. Post World War II priests of the secular city had even less sacristy chores to do and, while articulate about the deficiencies of the system, were not very creative in "making community." Even parishes fortunate enough to hold energetic and apostolic priests for a healthy time-period were not guaranteed after their death or transfer a comparable supply of quality performers. Lately the nuns, on whom for the greater part of the century a major part of the production-work of the Church fell, have been working out of parishes, rather than in them.

The management of the Church has fallen to such a low estate that increasingly senior priests no longer wish to be pastors. Young curates no longer seem content with a mere neighborhood ministry. And no one in authority seems equipped to see that the daily grind of home and hospital calls, long hours in office, school, or confessional, vital contacts with altar boys, teen-age societies, married couple groups, takes place, to say nothing of the parish dances, boat rides, and football leagues, which once were symbols of parish vitality. The basic influence is always personal knowledge of people in the district. This comes of service given again and again. The sheep of the fold follow that kind of shepherd. Yet it has been a long time since bishops expected priests to work seven days a week, if need be. Now the system is more concerned about his happiness than his sacerdotal productivity. Rectories and institutions have become centers of hospitality and personal fulfillment. Therapy for the bruised ego takes precedence over the pastoral mission. Gathering people into the fold by hard work is the exception rather than the rule. Priests assemble for interminable discussions on how to reach people, how to teach children, how to communicate with each other and superiors, but less and less are people reached, children taught, or superiors respected. Mass attendance is down, so are school enrollments and conversions. Badly married Catholics are in no rush to see the priest. Nor are priests any longer rushing around to do something about bad marriages. Some priests even think "fixing marriages" is unimportant. Saving the world is the thing, not souls. Bishops sit idly watching this deterioration continue. If they have increasing difficulty getting Catholic support for saving the world, it is for the reason that there are less and less committed constituents out there. Juniors in the system continue to talk about the need for new structures. The more serious sickness, however, is that time-tested structures are not functioning because bishops do not insist that priests and nuns work them the way the Church set them up. If Catholic priests today have little influence on the commonweal, it is because their ties with the faithful are weak. Ask the local politicians.

This depressing description has perhaps been oversimplified to overstress the point that the poor can be helped only by a powerful Church. The powerful Church is the result of the kind of efforts no longer consistently expended. Commentators in the East, South, Middle West and West of the country vary in their evaluations of contemporary pastoral effectiveness. Interpretation is always conditioned by the ideology and experience of the critic. Granting these variations and disagreements, this writer contends that the disasters experienced by the Church in dealing with the new poor—Blacks, Hispanics, Southern White—are the direct result of the breakdown of work habits of pastoral ministers of the Church. No voluntary institution in the United States has the money, the staff, such useful services as the Catholic Church. But those responsible for the care and improvement of the system have permitted the machinery to corrode. Parts were not replaced, training of staff became inferior, executive positions were filled on the basis of cronyism, sympathy, or by the book. Top management became increasingly fascinated with any cause save the well-being of its own internal system.

Blacks and Chicanos occasionally attribute the failure of the Church in their ghettos to racism. Racist feelings can never be discounted, although earlier minorities were readily called "Shanty," "Dagoes" or "Lunkheads" by their own priests. One funny chancellor recently answered a complaint about the mistreatment of a black parishioner by responding: "You have it all wrong. Our pastors do not mistreat blacks. They mistreat everybody." The hard fact, which few want to face, is that, while relations between clergy and laity were never always cordial, the earlier poor were gathered into a system with a clear purpose, whose managers made the system work. The new poor live in parishes without the discipline and quality of personnel necessary for effective response to their problems. The would-be leader of any social cause obtains his political power first by doing pedestrian things. Only dreamers set goals which the people cannot reach, or try to build a rooftop for shouting before they laid a brick on the ground floor.

Parishes must become what basically they are—localized assemblies of the faithful. The first job of the parish is to make people faithful to the Church. Except for a few mystics, this Church is the only Christ people will meet this side of the New Jerusalem. A weak Church can be a voice crying in the wilderness, but sensible leaders never set out to chop down trees in the jungle of urban life without the proper tools. When the church is a church of the faithful it is in a position to refashion the secular order with some hope of success. Until that day is likely, social activism against the bombing of Haiphong Harbor or the pardon of Richard Nixon had better be left to the politicians, whose politics are usually better than their morals. Rats running all over the neighborhood, heatless tenements in sub-zero weather, bartenders paying off cops for the privilege of dispensing drugs, a do-nothing local politician, are issues of community life in the ghetto and issues for the parish.

Advocacy of Church involvement in community issues presumes proper use of Catholic power. One man's mistake is another's cunning. There is no one right answer, certainly no one Catholic answer for everything. Normally, people and priests together ought to proceed on most things without a Vatican endorsement. They are as entitled to their share of mistakes as anyone else. However, when the public support of the Church is sought on a controversial matter of major moment, the judgment ought to be as right as a human decision can be. The Church on the line should talk for rights, not power, for public good, not special interests. Those who make a career of making fools of themselves hedge their bets some times by making a fool of the Church too. Some social movements, for example, are violence prone, and so are their leaders. Additionally, distilled hatred, misuse of sacred persons, places, and things are taken as the normal course for some Catholic activists. There is madness in the world and Moynihan thinks that intellectuals "have done a good deal to encourage and publicize this kind of madness."[5] When "my social cause right or wrong" becomes an ideology the extremists have a field day. Good causes lose their appeal and cause because senseless leaders turn off the very people who have the power to remedy the bad condition.

This explains why strong leadership is always vital to social movements. Corporate unity against the common enemy is necessary, which explains why the unionized workers deify labor leaders, the Irish protect their own, and blacks cover up for blacks. But only strong leadership can keep "the wild ones" in check. John Does will not long endure violence, tolerate the misuse of cathedrals or the abuse of the bishop. Some machinery must exist and someone, a priest if necessary, must prevent otherwise good people from menacing their own interests. Their iniquity only compounds the evil they fight. Priests and religious by profession ought to be steadying influences, not swordsmen. Every society wants things done in orderly fashion. Peter Berger insists (1) that "order is the primary imperative of social life," (2) "the forces of order are always stronger than those of disorder" and (3) "there are fairly narrow limits to the toleration of disorder in any human society."[6] If politicians know this, religious should not have to be told.

When all is said and done very few people will be happy about anything the Church does on the street. The secular world is willing to let ecclesiastics preach from the pulpit about prayer, sex, and stealing, but violent opposition always develops whenever they talk on the street about wage or interest rates, collective bargaining, union corruption, school bussing. It makes little difference what side they take. The more serious problem is to remain Catholic, even if on a particular issue the wrong side is chosen. But how to be truly Catholic? Today when two or three theologians are gathered together, God may be in the other room. Popes and bishops have a good deal to say which is authentically Catholic, but they do not please conservatives or liberals, poor or rich, Republicans or Democrats, Black or White. The most awesome enemy of religious intervention in society is government. Charles Whelan, a Jesuit legal expert, recently warned about the possible need against government of an "uphill, laborious and expensive fight for the equal protection of Catholics."[7] Catholic institutions which have eaten the golden apple of government money now find the Blessed Sacrament removed from their chapels, the crucifixes taken off the walls, and in giving service are under pressure to discriminate against Catholics. The Chief Justice of the Supreme Court on June 28, 1971 turned away aid for non-public school children because Catholics might use the freed money to upset the public school monopoly of American education, apparently an unconscionable act.[8]

To counterbalance myopic confidence in the ability of government to solve all the poor's problems, therefore, it is important to stress community activity by and for the poor. The *National Welfare Rights Organization,* the *Southern Christian Leadership Conference,* and the *Urban Coalition* are better known efforts in this direction, even though each of them experiences faction between local and national interests. A national lobby is sometimes offered as the best friend of the poor, but local actionists want problems met where they are felt "and less globe-trotting and speech-making."[9] Groups like the Catholic Church, centralized and decentralized at the same time, have a special contribution to make because they value government without being dominated by government.

The poor must realize that the government, except for its own bureaucracy, cannot make jobs. New jobs are made by farmers, inventors, businessmen, salesmen, traders. With all its job corps, youth corps, vocational training, the only jobs it can "create" are nonproductive public service titles which cost money raised from taxes, collected even from the poor. A generation ago the percentage of the population working for government was ten percent; it is now seventeen. Parkinson's Law[10]—bureaucrats multiply even when the work for which they were invented disappears—operates best in government enterprise for the simple reason that the government can go broke but it never goes out of business. The Church, better than anyone else, can harness people to exercise power on their own behalf. More prosperous groups do not always realize how much the poor are forced to stand on their two feet.

NOTES FOR CHAPTER FIVE

1 Herbert J. Gans, *The Urban Villagers*, (New York: Free Press, 1962.) For a description of family life in this community see pp. 45-57.

2 Bell, *op. cit.*, p. 426.

3 Governor Carey was then a Brooklyn congressman and the late Msgr. Molloy was the head of Catholic education in Brooklyn.

4 Nathan Glazer and Daniel P. Moynihan, *Beyond the Melting Pot*, Cambridge, Massachusetts: MIT Press, 1970, p. XVIII.

5 *Ibid.*, p. LXXXVII.

6 Peter L. Berger, "Sociology and Freedom," *The American Sociologist*, 1971, vol. 6 (February), pp. 3-4.

7 Charles Whelan, "Equal Protection for Catholics," *America*, November 9, 1974, p. 274.

8 Supreme Court of the United States, no. 87, October Term, 1970, *Alton L. Lemon et. al.* vs. David H. Kurtzman, as Superintendent of Public Instruction of the Commonwealth of Pennsylvania, et. al., June 28, 1971, Justice Warren Burger delivering the opinion of the court.

9 For a summary of the woes facing these organizations see an article by Ernest Holsendolph, "Social Action Hit By Financial Woes," *New York Times*, November 8, 1974, p. 20.

10 C. Northcote Parkinson, *Parkinson's Law*, Boston: Houghton Mifflin, 1957, pp. 33-34.

CHAPTER SIX

THE GOVERNMENT COUNTS, BUT SO DO CORPORATE MANAGERS

"The Question to be asked is not what business can do for the poor but what can people who manage business do? When we talk about business responsibility for the poor, this is not something handed down from a board room on high. Business is people. So we ask instead: What can business executives do for the poor?"

WALTER HOOKE
Director of Personnel
United Parcel Service

The common assumption underlying all American discussion of poverty is that government is the chief agent of reform. The right side of the political spectrum, as much as those on the left, presume this. One side may make different proposals than the other, but somehow each relies on government to provide the final answer. Franklin Roosevelt is blithely credited with a credo that goes back at least to the "Guardians" of Plato's *Republic*. More recently, Emile Durkheim's world-view presumed the same thing. The rhetoric of private enterprisers grandiloquently flowing from the lips of labor leaders, farm leaders, chairmen of boards, says one thing, but political potentates, protected labor, subsidized agriculture, regulated business, practice more like constituent elements of a highly corporate state. Even intellectuals operate as if answers to economic and social problems can alone or finally be found in some Washington bureaucracy or government "think tank."[1]

It must be admitted that government or the state, as it is frequently called, is the part of society which gets done those things which help living together seem better than living apart. It does what people usually cannot do for themselves. "The sum total of those conditions of social living whereby men are enabled to achieve their own integral perfection more fully and more easily" is the common good, of which, according to John XXIII,[2] government is the supreme protector. In Catholic thought the ambit of government authority is wide, because presumptively its officers, though elected by plurality or majority, represent all the people. Indeed, there are not wanting those who maintain that the Church might have preempted the word "socialism" for its own use had Marxists not stained it with the stigma of materialism, class conflict, and irreligion. In aiding a people's pursuit of social justice the Church permits wide scope to government.[3] For Popes, therefore, governments are not natural enemies of the people or the Church. Even though some human needs will be left unsatisfied and perfect happiness will escape everyone, government acts responsibly when it makes it easier for people to exercise their rights and do their duty. But what does this mean in the concrete? Papal encyclicals are not marching orders for Catholics. Nor are they a pocket of planks for a political platform.[4] The moral norms contained therein—including the assertion that government has a special role from God, if you will, to coordinate social affairs— must be applied by peoples who vary in their historical development and who may be in serious conflict among themselves about the most desirable course for their government to follow.

A good case study of sound principles leading in different directions can be drawn from John XXIII's *Pacem in Terris*, hailed by all as the final gift of his wisdom to mankind. The jolly pope argues that, while governments should not show preferences to any one civic group,

> considerations of justice and equity, however, can at times demand that those involved in civil government give more attention to the less fortunate members of the community, since they are less able to defend their rights and to assert their legitimate claims.[5]

This certainly is a valid interpretation of a social justice. What people need but are unable to get through no fault of their own, society ought to provide—food, medical care, shelter, and so forth. This principle is the basis of all social welfare programs and the rationale used by social actionists to move government agencies to do more for the poor than presently is done. The principle is valid and unimpeachable.

But then later on in the same encyclical in speaking of government protection for minority groups, John XXIII adds this caveat:

> Minority groups either because of a reaction to their present situation or because of their historical difficulties are often inclined to exalt beyond due measure anything proper to their own people, so as to place themselves above human values.[6]

He goes on to indicate that minorities, whose very assets have developed under peculiar circumstances, can develop their culture even further by dealing properly with the majority, but not "if they sow discord, which can cause considerable damage."[7] Here is a typical admonition for which the Church is famous, and which in the light of experience Popes are eminently justified in giving. Practical judgments are good or bad, opportune or inopportune, productive or unproductive. They cannot be made except by "those who live and work in the specific sectors of human society in which the problems arise."[8] Neither idealist nor pragmatist, as long as they both seem to be moving in the right direction, are essentially the last word on a subject.

This is very apropos to conditions in the United States, where government responds to problems by moving about as far and as quickly as the value system and the insight of the voters permit. The parameters of licit policy are set not by abstract norms but by the value system and the fears in the ascendancy at a given time.

For example, on the question of redistribution of income, Americans can move with relative ease from one ethical principle to a second without seeming to realize principles frequently conflict. One norm says: "All men, rich and poor, having been born equal, may freely pursue their own ideal of happiness." The second maxim prescribes "Whatever men ultimately get, they have earned by competence and hard work." It is hard to say with authority whether John Locke, Thomas Jefferson or the Protestant Ethicians put these ideas together but they do remain the essential components of the American Dream. The Founding Fathers, whoever they are, made a big thing out of opportunity for success and success itself. Money somehow was associated with opportunity and reward. Then money became might, and might meant God's favor. Charles Beard's interpretation of the constitution may have been superseded[9] but his stress on the importance of economics to the American way of life is still valid. Even the rise of organized labor to co-equal status with business receives a blessing because it is earned economic power.[10] Consequently, in the American ethos everything kneels before the vicissitudes of the business cycle, education and culture, arts and religion, public works and public protection. Those who wish to share in the gains and losses, according to the old dream, do so starting from the place which they are assigned to occupy.[11]

The society described by these previous remarks is probably on its way out. Commentators of the contemporary scene, like Walter Rostow, Daniel Bell or David Riesman now speak of the "post-industrial society."[12] Once upon a time industrial society was involved simply in producing and distributing goods. This was what wealth, even the poor man's wealth, was all about. The rules of that game may still apply to emerging nations, but not to the highly successful nations. Why not? Because people in places like the United States, West Germany or Japan, no longer are satisfied with mere production and distribution of goods. They have plenty of economic goods, more than they really need. New psychological needs, new status needs, new quests for religious experience demand satisfaction. Managing these ever expanding appetites of the masses for satisfactions only indirectly related to money, is the newer challenge. At the turn of the century the most respected and cursed men in society were producers of wealth. The faces of J. P. Morgan, Andrew Carnegie, Commodore Vanderbilt, Henry Ford, Thomas Edison were familiar to the poor. Who knows the ten wealthiest men in America today? The populace knows more about Henry Kissinger, Dean Rusk, Robert McNamara than the millionaire presidents of the giant corporations.

Status in American society is moving from those who produce wealth for the satisfaction of needs to those who provide service for the satisfaction of wants. White-collar workers—the men of service—now outnumber blue-collar workers—the producers—42-30 million.[13] The fastest growing occupational group in the country is the technical-managerial class. Those who price the cost of beef on the hoof, set tax rates for government, guide missiles around the world are more admired than ranchers, taxpayers, or dye-makers. They have become central to decision makers in government and business, and even to generals who wish to win a war.

Professional influence on government is a matter of special concern. By definition they are the men who have unraveled the mysteries of nature and society.[14] Because they believe everything can always be done better, they are not partial to the way things were done yesterday. For the technical scientist nothing is normal or natural. Today's norm exists only until a better one is devised. It is not surprising, therefore, that so many intellectuals in recent years have affiliated themselves, emotionally if not philosophically, with the radical left of American society, which for other reasons wants continuous change until arrival at Utopia or the pure Communal State. One of the fascinating paradoxes of our time is, as Daniel Bell suggests that

> the workers, whose grievances were once the driving energy for social change, are more satisfied with the society than the intellectuals.[15]

In fact the leaders of workingmen's associations and many elected officials look upon professionals with suspicion. David Halberstam has the classic example of this in the retort of Speaker Rayburn to Vice-President Johnson's glowing description of the brilliance of McGeorge Bundy, Dean Rusk and Robert McNamara's performance at the first meeting of the Kennedy Cabinet.

Well, Lyndon, you may be right and they may be as intelligent as you say, but I'd feel a whole lot better about them if one of them had run for sheriff once.[16]

It is one of Halberstam's minor theses that "the brightest" put America into the mudholes of Vietnam.

The special problem seems to be that in their critical assessment of society and their assertion of power over the direction of change, intellectuals have adopted the Hispanics and Blacks, and to a lesser extent the white poor, as allies. The new minorities are natural foils for smart complainers. First, the bright men articulate better the nature of the poor man's grievances. Secondly, economic ladder-climbing is not so easy any more. Unskilled and semi-skilled workers are in short demand. Society needs fewer of them and that means fewer jobs for the poor. Idea-men, scientists, technicians, administrators, on the other hand, are in short supply. Consequently, upward mobility is likely to come not from brawn but from brain, not from economics as from education.

The advocates of government control of this managerial revolution are already sniping at the old ethic which gave prizes to achievers. As a matter of fact, the suggestion is being made that competition is immoral because the losers are made to feel that they are born losers. The new ethicians want society to guarantee more than opportunity. They want society to guarantee everyone equality of achievement. But how can society distribute its prizes equally? What is the formula or the mechanism? In a competitive majoritarian society, no group with winning numbers will ever redistribute away its hard-earned gains, certainly not by taxation. This is a fact of democratic life. Yet radical economic thinkers argue that society must do precisely that, must limit or nullify the social power of the majority voting bloc, whenever society (or someone) decides it is inimical to the well-being of the country. This argumentation is a throwback to the nullification theory of John C. Calhoun, who demanded for slave states the right to nullify oppressive federal laws. Proposals to establish a veto power in subgroups over majoritarian domination are based on this thinking.[17]

Daniel Bell rationalizes the case as follows:

Socialism has had political appeal for a century now not so much because of its moral depiction of what future society would be like, but because of material disparities within disadvantaged classes, the hatred of bourgeois society by many intellectuals, and the eschatological vision of a "cunning" of history. The normative ethic was only implicit; never spelled out and justified. The claim for "equality of result" is a socialist ethic (as equality of opportunity is the liberal ethic) and as a moral basis for society it can finally succeed in obtaining men's allegiance not by material reward but by philosophical justification. An effort in politics has to be confirmed in philosophy. And an attempt to provide that confirmation is now underway.[18]

The old meritocratic order—the rule by individual merit—is slowly being argued out of existence in favor of a new order of enforced social equity. Future rewards by fiat are to be allocated to those who have been disadvantaged through no fault of their own. For example, women, Blacks and Chicanos in proportion to their numbers have special claims on employment. Henceforth, the principle of merit is to be made subordinate to the principle of proportionate reward. No longer is opportunity the issue. Not even discrimination. Representation and participation by those with reasonable claims on society is to be a determining principle of social allocation. And so minority quotas, a concept at least as old as John Stuart Mill, becomes the lever of progress.[19]

The obvious end result of this principle-in-action is a corporative state of some kind. If argued out in the market-place of ideas or in the market-place itself, managed democracy may result in better attention to the remaining disadvantages in American society. But if the social allocation of rewards becomes a basic function of government, class conflicts will become exacerbated at a rate hitherto unknown in our society. Since government is not society but only one arm of society, its basic job is to balance the relations of all divergent interests. Power used to flatten society by fiat usually makes all men poor in more ways than one.

The failure of the Great Society itself to provide all the answers, while providing some, has lately called into question the infallibility of government bureaucrats. For one thing, hard working citizens discovered that large chunks of their income were poured into a non-productive pork barrel. For another, the poor are still walking an economic treadmill, even though they have been led to expect great things. Even cabinet officers and their university advisers confess without embarrassment that certain answers are just not there. It is not surprising, therefore, that a lot of people have begun to give another hopeful look at American business and in response corporate executives have begun to sound like social workers.

This is not surprising. In spite of political oratory, corporations are no longer run by robber barons. Business enterprise cannot any more be simply equated with property, manufacturing and distribution of goods. The network of relationships among people who share the common life of business, and upon which society depends for its well-being, is one of our fundamental social institutions. More and more corporate life, not family, town, or Church, is where people find identity and fulfillment. Even married women are discovering the excitement and importance, to say nothing of the money, from being in business. Without question the corporation can be an instrument of dull deeds, but, as Elton Mayo discovered almost a half century ago, it is an arena too of initiative, creativity, and togetherness.[20]

So, when a public issue such as poverty becomes a matter of general concern, or when discussions about the redistribution of income reaches the hot point, corporations and their managers are going to have a great deal to say. American business has long since moved away from classic dollars-and-cents management, mostly because in the newer political economy they control only one-third of the final votes, with labor and public partners sitting on the rest. Even if corporate managers were—as some undoubtedly are—the self-serving pirates of old, their power to act is legitimated only in a tri-partite decision-making process. Regardless of motive they see social gains as helpful to ongoing money gains. Collective decisions "often vitiate the individual's desires" as Daniel Bell insists tirelessly.[21] But this only proves that businessmen have a veto power of their own. They may not be able to solve the problems of the poor, but the poor will never really be helped without them.

Walter Hooke thinks that abstractions such as "management" are not constructive. He would rather talk of "managerial persons." Management must show a profit and balance the accounts, but "managerial persons" have the social conscience or its lack. Hooke assigns three kinds of influence to these people: (1) over company policy; (2) on company practices; (3) on the character of the people who work for them.[22]

Making Company Policy

Many companies have no particular social policy. They make their product and sell it period. As long as that remains the rule business effort on behalf of the poor is likely to be minimal. Other firms are socially conscious and their success helps hospitals, universities, government, which being non-competitive live at someone else's expense. But their policy precludes executive involvement in social controversy because it is seen as "bad for business." Because public opinion is fickle, frequently unjust, losing sales or going out of business for an idealistic cause does not seem to make business sense. This probably explains why Chambers of Commerce and their constituents have given very little vigorous public support to private religious education. To appear unfriendly to the established American system of public education would in their view be bad for business, even though privately they endorse religious education, and often draw preferred junior executives from local Catholic universities.

No one should object to business deciding what creates good will in the public forum or what is likely to pay off in new customers. But, the philosophical question is: What is a right decision? Managers have to learn like everyone else what are the social decisions compatible with profit-making. Trial and error are involved. On the other hand, decisions also reflect a value system and people's character. There is something regressive and timorous, for example, in the failure of private enterprise to give large public support to the largest private educational system in the world, especially since a majority of the public and political office holders endorse not only the existence but government support of this private endeavor. Businessmen, however, dread hostility from the afficionados of public education and from American intellectuals, whose anti-Catholic school bias blankets much of the media, where business sells its goods.

The manner in which managers reconcile these tensions is indicative of their social conscience. No one really expects businessmen to be leading social crusaders. Labor leaders are not. Heads of families are not. Churchmen ought to be when the issue is fundamental. Intellectuals are likely to be, because their appetite for dissent is insatiable, and they will always have tenure. But wide areas of movement are possible even for the most cautious man, providing he is pointed in the right direction. Whatever uncertainty businessmen have about what they ought to be doing for Catholic education, they ought with assurance to be doing something for the poor—because at the very least they are potential employees, whose lack of skill or poor industrial habits will ultimately mean bad business for some of them.

This is the point at which the right managers convince bosses that the really bad thing for business is the aggravated social problems, that affirmative action on behalf of the poor can be good for business. People who work in board-rooms are not always aware of the conditions on the first floor of the firm, or even in the city where they earn their daily bread. One level in company development is reached when companies learn not to use their power to block necessary improvements. Maturity comes when corporations bring about or participate in human betterment. Take, for example, the case of unionization of employees. Philip Murray once wryly remarked that hostile managers beget hostile labor leaders. Collective bargaining can be a nuisance to the industrial autocrat and it creates a fair share of labor tyrants. But it does uplift living standards and stabilizes industry without destroying profits. The garment industry has been the classic showcase for blessings associated with collective bargaining. Even in seasonal industries, established firms like Coca Cola can successfully work out a contract in Florida with United Farm Workers which gives the company both work-force stability and high productivity. The farm workers get what they rarely get anywhere—year round wages, sanitary labor camps, and the opportunity to buy company built homes.[23]

Open-mindedness or at least sensible concession to the community sense of right and wrong is another essential ingredient of good management. Corporations need this because, wherever they exist, they exercise considerable political power. They control costly land and equipment, employ thousands or hundreds as the case may be, and their success or failure is important to the town or city in which they do business. How they exercise a social role is the clue to the credit or blame they receive.

Even when companies are limited in potential, usually because of size, better than most they can offer scholarships for poor children, subsidize at least in part self-help programs in poverty areas, initiate job training to encourage the upward movement of their own employees and, above all, expose their executives to programs of social awareness.

What Counts Is The Job

The biggest single resource of any company with respect to the poor is still the job opportunity. Businessmen are more correct than most when they unsentimentally turn the question of poverty around to the ways and means by which the unemployed become truck-drivers, mail carriers, and mechanics. Jobs with good pay alone provide the poor with a decent standard of living and ipso facto a modicum of decency. Talented farmers' sons, migrating to the city, frequently find employment—because they take jobs no one else wants and are used to hard work. Expanding regions of the country attract talent merely by offering bonus wage scales.[24] But within the urban jungle what can be done for the square pegs unsuited to the round holes on the employment board? The picture is at times so distressing that some of the poor give up filing applications at all.

Managers make a contribution to the relief of this problem

when they aggressively reach out for the recruits no one seems to want and when they fit them to the opportunity. Job fairs in high schools and community buildings, mobile recruiting offices brought directly into poverty areas, are the tools of socially conscious managers, who soon discover that poor are poor not so much because they lack talent, but because they have been badly taught. Management officials, like military officers, ask why they must supply for the deficiencies of public education. But since inferior education, even of the middle class, has become a fact of American life, the social function of business is to take the burden upon itself. Another forgotten piece of data is that the vast army of poor include those who were born poor, the handicapped, the blind, the deaf, the lame; those who became poor by illness or youthful misadventures which led them into drug addiction or even to jail. Corporations working with agencies such as *Lighthouse* and *Abilities Incorporated* diminish the price of being handicapped by offering jobs tailored to persons. The *Kemper Insurance Company of Chicago,* in association with the Illinois Drug Abuse Program, has had satisfactory results with rehabilitated drug addicts. *Polaroid* in New England pre-tests and pre-trains convicts prior to release as part of an employment policy which it calls successful. The name of the social game—for vast thousands—is and must be rehabilitation and re-education.

The results of these outreach efforts by *United Parcel Service* have been described by Walter Hooke.

We hired a black Chicagoan in 1965 who at the time of employment earned $2,600. Last year he earned $20,396.30 driving a trailer out of his home city. In Georgia we took on a white union member whose salary was $3,244 a year in 1969. He now earns $18,423.84. In 1972 we hired a black man who was earning $7,000 in Georgia, a fairly decent pay at the time and place. Last year he earned $16,000. In January 1971 a black in Alabama in four years has moved from $1,560 to $16,430.86. These are only some of the answers which business can provide to problems of poverty.[25]

Obviously, the poor man who succeeds learns more from job

training than mere technique. He learns good work habits, discipline, responsibility, ambition, even simple things like punctuality, the qualities he needs to succeed in the world of work. Ordinarily the family provides the necessary socialization. But, as James Coleman of Johns Hopkins University once discovered while doing research for the federal government and much to the dismay of the national educational bureaucracy, bad family background and inferior social class make equal education a myth, no matter how equal the schools seem to be.[26] Long before the Coleman report, businessmen accepted this as a fact of life. Supportive services provided by management—high school equivalency courses, counseling, disciplined work units— were invented precisely to supply for this deficiency in background. Though costly and at times irritating to the immediate supervisors of slow learners, top management in large corporations realizes that the alternative to this kind of affirmative action is doom through generations for large quantities of citizens. The principle of redress rationalizing training programs has been formulated by John Rawls:

> Those, whoever they are, may gain from their good fortune only on terms that improve the situation of those who have lost out.[27]

By all accounts the progress is noticeable.

This tug of war between Christian humanism and good business comes to an easy end when managers make a personal commitment to the special care of those who through no fault of their own are disadvantaged in life. That conversion, if you will, has its impact on how corporate power is used on behalf of causes which seem to have little connection with normal business operations. Big business can use income to support institutions and firms which are poor-oriented. Where company money is deposited, where the regional office is built, can make a big difference. Corporate patronage is more important than political patronage, because it is productive of wealth and income for the poor through sales and jobs. Enterprises, such as *Levi-Strauss*, require their general contractors to obtain competitive bids from minority-group firms. This stimulates group pride as much as it stimulates business in the right areas.

Over and above jobs and money, the next great asset of a corporation is talent. Without exception, not excluding universities, American corporations are surfeited with the country's best brains and best organizers. Those who achieve or maintain economic positions have ability. It takes talent to manage anything that depends for survival on showing a profit. Failure is more noticeable in business than in the Church, government, or education because the taskmaster is stern. It is corporate personnel on a full or part time loan to a given community that can be essential to the success of some project meaningful to poor people. Organizing a cooperative, teaching cost control, demonstrating the effective methods of obtaining federal funding or foundation grants, creating health and welfare programs, day care centers, homes for the aged, these are things which corporation executives do for a living and which can be done at company expense for a cause. Dollar-a-year men go to Washington but can go to the ghetto too. Many recreation centers, which serve the poor, owe their existence to funding, property and licenses arranged by businessmen.

The use of this executive talent to train people to help themselves, to instruct them in techniques of efficiency, to deal with government agencies, may be the most important service by business. The very skills by which business operates at a profit are the skills needed by poor people to survive. Communities need to know where to go to demand garbage pickup, insect control, street lights, food stamps, social security payments, tax advice, vocational counselling, summer camps, recreational programs. Self-help programs properly conceived and managed provide the skills and the knowledge.

There are some basic limits to what a company can do to put an end to poverty, even in its own community. Because money must be made for owners and workers, it cannot be expended on "causes" indefinitely. Well established companies, usually large and consistently profitable, have a greater capacity to promote ambitious social action programs from which economic return may be negligible. Smaller firms usually can expect some economic return from costly job training programs, e.g., new employees with a higher level of expected productivity, and even gain in prestige from the furlough of executives to social organizations. But the deadliest fact to be faced is that a company's ability to engage in constructive social action will be determined by what happens in the marketplace. Social reform is costly and must be paid for either in higher taxes or higher prices. In one way or another social reform becomes a problem for consumers.

NOTES FOR CHAPTER SIX

1 For the latest statement of this ethos see Richard J. Whalen, *A Personal View of America from Kennedy to Nixon to Kennedy,* (New York: Houghton-Mifflin, 1974.)

2 John XXIII, *Pacem in Terris,* (New York: Paulist, 1963), (no. 58), p. 23.

3 Jeremiah Newman, *Change in the Catholic Church,* (Baltimore: Helicon, 1965), pp. 179-181.

4 For a good review of a Catholic controversy over the authority and meaning of John XXIII's *Mater et Magistra* see Garry Wills' *Politics and Catholic Freedom,* (Chicago: Henry Regnery, 1964).

5 John XXIII, *loc. cit.,* (no. 56), p. 23.

6 John XXIII, *loc. cit.,* (no. 97), p. 35.

7 *Ibid.*

8 *Ibid.,* (no. 160), p. 55.

9 Charles Beard, *An Economic Interpretation of the Constitution,* (New York: Macmillan, 1941).

10 Derek C. Bok and John T. Dunlop, *Labor and the American Community,* (New York: Simon and Schuster, 1970), p. 6.

11 See Richard Henry Tawney, *The Acquisitive Society,* (New York: Harcourt, Brace, 1920), ch. 6.

12 W. W. Rostow, *Stages of Economic Growth,* translated by B. Marschenko, (Preger, 1961). David Reisman, *Mass Leisure,* (Glencoe, Illinois: Free Press, 1958). Guild Socialist, Arthur J. Penty, as far back as World War I described this kind of society as collectivist and servile: See *Old Worlds for New: A Study of the Post-Industrial State,* (London: G. Allen & Unwin, 1917).

13 *Technology and the American Economy,* Report of the National Commission on Technology etc., vol. 1, Washington, D.C., Superintendent of Documents, 1966, p. 30.

14 Talcott Parsons, "Professions," *International Encyclopedia of Social Sciences,* (New York: Macmillan, 1968), vol. 12.

15 Daniel Bell, *The End of Ideology,* (Glencoe, Illinois: Free Press, 1960), p. 375.

16 David Halberstam, *The Best and the Brightest,* (Greenwich, Connecticut: Fawcett Publication, 1969), p. 53.

17 James McGregor Burns, *The Deadlock of Democracy,* (New Jersey: Englewood Cliffs, Prentice Hall, 1963), p. 57.

18 Daniel Bell, *The Coming of Post-Industrial Society,* (New York: Basic Books, 1973), p. 433.

19 John Stuart Mill, *On Liberty, Representative Government,* (London: Oxford University), pp. 247-271.

20 The entire human relations phase of American business management began with the discovery of how group affiliation or disaffiliation in business was the most important key to productivity. See Elton Mayo, *The Human Problem of an Industrial Civilization,* (Boston: Harvard University Graduate School of Business Administration, 1933), and his *The Social Problems of an Industrial Civilization,* (Boston: Harvard University Graduate School of Business Administration, 1945). Somewhat later William H. Whyte in his *The Organization Man,* (New York: Simon and Schuster, 1956), p. 3, wrote about these men "who have left home, spiritually as well as physically, to take the vows of organization (i.e., corporate) life."

21 Daniel Bell, *The Coming of Post-Industrial Society,* p. 283.

22 A paper entitled "Management Programs of Social Reform" presented at St. John's University, New York City, May 14, 1974.

23 Don Cardtz, "Corporate Farming A Tough Road to Hoe," *Fortune,* August 1972, pp. 135-139.

24 Robert J. Lampman, *Ends and Means of Reducing Income Poverty,* (Chicago: Markham, 1971), ch. 5.

25 Data provided by Mr. Walter Hooke at St. John's University, May 14, 1974.

26 James Coleman, *Equality of Educational Opportunity,* (Washington, D. C., U. S. Office of Education, 1966). For a critique of this report see Frederick Mosteller and Daniel P. Moynihan, *On Equality of Educational Opportunity,* (New York: Vintage, 1972).

27 John Rawls, *A Theory of Justice,* (Cambridge, Mass.: Harvard University, 1971), p. 101.

CHAPTER SEVEN

NO STATE OWNERSHIP OF THE POOR

"There are many things Christians ought to be doing for the poor. One of the things we ought not to be doing is encouraging state ownership of the poor. The more we take from Caesar the more we have to render him."

MISS DOROTHY DAY

"I have often wondered if the Congressional Chaplain should not appear for prayer at the end of the daily session rather than at the beginning so that the members might better meditate on what was achieved that day in terms of the lofty ideals proclaimed at the opening hour."

HON. HUGH L. CAREY
GOVERNOR OF NEW YORK

Dorothy Day defines a revolutionary differently from everyone else. Most people hearing the word conjure up an image of a man with a gun, or a political assassin about to use nitro on the White House. But the patron saint of the Catholic Worker Movement thinks the true revolutionary is the person who in the name of Jesus Christ turns over his life to the service of the poor. The man or woman who makes the Sermon on the Mount his or her own special gospel, who turns the other cheek or walks the other mile as needed, is the one who turns his world upside down.

Central to the faith of a Catholic Worker is the belief that the coat hanging in the closet belongs as a matter of right to the poor. Few theologians would contest this statement as a valid interpretation of the gospel narrative. It has been a common Catholic tradition from the beginning that property, while held privately, is intended for the common benefit of all, not just for the owner.

The communitarian strain in Catholicism is so deep that no one would accuse of theft the poor man in dire needs who took of someone else's surplus to survive. Dorothy Day would deem it better that the Christian with a surplus dispense it to the poor on his own initiative.

Fellow Catholics are sometimes bemused by this moral absolutism, a few are annoyed. While there are not wanting those who breathe a sigh of relief when Houses of Hospitality are founded in neighboring parishes and dioceses, most bishops and most Catholics have encouraged, rarely discouraged, the apostolate for which Dorothy Day has become justly famous. The adherents are looked upon generally as idealistic witnesses of Christ in a craven world, or sometimes as bumbling dreamers having little impact either on the Catholic conscience or the capitalistic society. Nonetheless, this small band of earthlings, striving to be saintly in Christ's mode, are a reminder of what the Church really is all about, and a far cry from secular revolutionaries who make headlines. Ordinarily, a revolutionary movement has a founder with a coterie whose driving force is anger, whose special weapon is violence. These footnoters of history tend to withdraw from the world or destabilize it. Not infrequently, their rule is more domineering and oppressive than the system they seek to overthrow. Some Catholic social movements, even the non-violent kind, lack spiritual motivation or a communal prayer life, so that the pressing goal is the Kingdom of Man, not Christ. The Catholic Worker Movement has never suffered from these defects, because its goals and methods and spirituality are truly Catholic.

Dorothy Day and her co-workers have made a significant contribution to Catholic thinking about the poor.

1. They serve to remind us that the poor are people, individual persons, not groups, blocs, and alliances, votes, or front page social items. Once asked "who are the poor" Miss Day gave another atypical answer:

The poorest people in the country are to be found in mental hospitals, old age homes, and prisons. The word poor should not be used in relation to those on the outside. The man who has freedom to be poor on a street corner or sleep in a doorway is less destitute than the one who is just parked away and over a period of many years just forgotten.[1]

This response indicates that there are various categories of poor, some of which are "more poor" than others. In contemporary culture, poverty is associated with lack of money or the absence of things which money can buy. This definition by itself does not suffice. Consequently, enlarging the budgets of protective institutions, which keep more people out than in, does not necessarily depauperize the residents or inmates. Denizens of the Bowery nowadays receive monthly checks from government but would remain just as poor if the amounts were doubled. Sociologists acknowledge that the present welfare system has the unintended effect of perpetuating poverty. The welfare poor have become caseloads, not people, for the simple reason that it just is not possible to administer a municipal outlay of one billion dollars, as is the situation in New York City, either on a family basis or with trust in the basic goodness of poor people. The investigative process, the eligibility requirements, the need for probative documents are governed necessarily by coldblooded bureaucratic procedures. An overburdened social worker has no time for personal attentions and society cannot afford to double the professional staff. These are inherent qualities of any government program which goes beyond distributing fixed insurance payments.

When voluntary effort proved inadequate to the size of the poverty problem, government assumed major responsibility, which is precisely what should have been done. But the record is now abundantly clear that government programs are extravagantly costly and lack the human touch. Partisans of socialized enterprises, not all of whom are Socialists, would, in spite of these obvious defects, governmentalize the entire welfare process further. Not only do entrenched bureaucrats of public corporations not want "their" money going to private agencies, but they resent the competition which enjoys respect for its honesty and productivity. Possibly the greatest danger to the effort to humanize welfare work is hostility to religious voluntary effort. Here is the nub of what is likely to be a major contemporary problem. Since the greatest single obstacle to a totally socialized state is the Church, any Church, the Church must be driven out of the public welfare business. And what easier way to accomplish this than to deny religious social agencies public money, which has been theirs from the beginning. Barbara Ward, a progressive lady of international repute and an advocate of proper government activity, makes this shrewd comment:

> The state is by nature so powerful and compelling and voracious an institution that the citizen standing alone against it is all but powerless. He needs counter-institutions, above all the counter-institution of the Church, which of all organized bodies alone can look Caesar in the face and claim a higher loyalty.[2]

Secular humanitarians are careful not to appear anti-religious. They probably believe that in a secularized society religious groups have little to offer anymore. But more likely they will, if they can, truly brook no opposition to their concept of an homogenized society, constructed on purely humanistic lines and engineered by their own special Vatican. They will manufacture hurdles for voluntary agencies, if need be. Entrenched publicly-financed religious hospitals, for example, are now under pressure to perform abortions, (euthanasia to follow), and Catholic adoption agencies have been sued because in the assignment of children the religious preference of prospective parents is a leading concern.

Perhaps the Church deserves credit for its own difficulties with the omni-competent state. For many centuries the Church gave absolute sacred meaning to enterprises connected with feeding the poor and curing the sick. These activities which alleviated the bodily distress of man became a soul-work performed mainly by people who dedicated themselves exclusively to religion. As the notion of sacred receded in history, the secular state reached out to take over these functions one by one and to declare them worldly deeds subject to the state, not the Church. One French writer capsulated this conversion of reality as follows:

The idea of a secular state could have risen only in a personalist civilization leavened by Christianity . . . It is the state
realizing the spiritual limits of its sovereignty.[3]

Concern for the growing giganticism of the state is not re-
stricted to Catholic revolutionaries like Dorothy Day, Catholic
intellectuals like Hilaire Belloc, or conservative economists like
Frederich Hayek or Ludwig Von Mises.[4] Admonitions against
merging the notion "state" and "society" (nation) into some in-
effable and everlasting marriage are many and ancient.[5] Frequently the warnings accompany the ascendancy of social planners to
government power. For a long time English as well as German
Socialists have worked toward a society totally organized by paid
employees of central government according to "scientific laws,"
even though the science of governing does not exist, while artists
of good governing follow no law but their own principles and
intuition.[6]

Popes—from Leo XIII to Paul VI—even though accused at
times of being revolutionary themselves by more conservative
Catholics,[7] have inveighed for generations against the socialist
state strictly defined. American Catholics, save those committed
to the perpetuation of economic privilege, have never been afraid
of government because, as George G. Higgins pointed out almost
a quarter of a century ago, "Big government, normally speaking, is
more or less a direct and inevitable consequence of economic liberalism."[8] This is to say that, when powerful social structures are
not up to the mark in serving people, who else can step in to protect the poor but government? But if American Catholic social
thought has stressed the importance of government legislation, it
is not because the Church believes this to be more important than
personalism. It means more likely that the social actionists have
written books which tickled the American fancy more than the
works of personalists. For this reason the name John A. Ryan
looms larger in American Catholic history than, for example, Paul
Hanly Furfey, although both were equally proliferous in promoting their particular slant on the social question.[9] It is a continued
paradox that the social reform message of Catholicism has drawn

more public attention than the personalist message. But, after two generations of social engineering, another look at the value of personalism is in order. The depression argument that government controls over the mass production of goods and services are necessary and now must be equally extended over education, welfare, religion deserves careful examination and limited application.

2. The second contribution of the Catholic Worker Movement to a renewed social order is its insistence that persons, not groups, have the first responsibility to provide succor for the poor in the order of their greatest need. Primary onus is not placed on the few who manage institutions, but on the many who acquiesce in other people's continued degrading poverty. Every system is a mechanism through which something gets done. Systems do many things better than individuals acting alone can do. But it is also true that once common purposes are institutionalized—e.g., social advance by achievement, income by wage rather than piece rates —then those who do not fit in with the system become deprived. Not only the underachievers, but also overachievers. Hard workers and competitors would rather be paid by the piece than by the week. This explains why compensating mechanisms are vital to society. Preserving human happiness must balance the efficient functioning of the institution. And for this people-effort is important, not only to make other people feel better, but to reorientate the social goals, if necessary. People make as many mistakes as the system, but their mistakes are not so costly and they are easily reversed. This is why private effort, when possible, is always preferable to government effort. Highly endowed foundations deal more realistically with the poor than government, which tends to throw its entire power to some extreme like Victorian rigorism or Humanistic sentimentalism. Cruel work houses or welfare corruption, poverty tests or government domination of collective bargaining are typical of the rigidity of the philosophy ruling the going state machinery. The cruelty of Uriah Heeps is somewhat obvious. But Huey Longs, who seem benevolent, may perform the unkindest service of all because, while seeming to give the poor all that they need, leave them with no new skills, no sense of responsibility for each other, not even hope.

One Harvard professor realizes the significance of realism in his remarks:

> The claims of the poor are, of course, among the oldest traditions in Western thought and are central to the idea of Christian love. But Christian love—charity as *caritas*—accepted the poor as worthy in themselves and loved the poor as poor without endowing them with higher qualities than they possessed. In that sense, classic Protestant liberalism—with its sympathy and humanitarianism, rather than love—corroded the social conscience of the Catholic world. From a different source, the romaticizing of the poor, a tradition going back to Villon, also led to the erosion of *caritas* toward poor.[10]

Dorothy Day says the same thing from experience with her poor.

> Romanticism about the poor, though it has a place in the lives of the young, is a dangerous thing. A personalism which misleads a young thing into dreaming that she and she alone can save this habitual drunkard can lead to tragedy. One college girl went overboard in her sense of personal responsibility by marrying such a person who five children later deserted the family by hanging himself.[11]

The chief value of making people responsible for people is that there is no middleman. From the days of the gospel, Christians find plausible excuses for not putting themselves on the line. Usually the fault lies elsewhere, in the wife, the new farm, or "the system." But if ever free enterprise had ample latitude for exercise, it is in this area of personal service to the poor. No one ever prevented St. Vincent de Paul from going to the galleys or Martin Luther King from going to jail. Prelates and presidents may have very good reason, and may be bound by law, to deny funds to poverty causes. But neither prelates nor presidents can prevent the celebration of the corporal and spiritual works of mercy. Everyone works for a system somewhere, if only to earn his daily bread or find a home. As a member of that system he is under the command of a social situation which he cannot control. But the doorway of personalist service is quite wide. There is the freedom to do what other people consider insane or imprudent. There is freedom to decide what the poor really need, not what some book says they ought to need. True *caritas* serves needs not wants, extends sympathy and support without stifling or debasing, goes out to their level but never down to their squalor. Christ was arrested because he was a "friend of the poor and sinners" but never because he toppled the Temple of Jerusalem. He wanted no part of anyone's plot to lop off an ear, even if the reason seemed good.

One of the hardest things for the personalist to do is to remember why he is a personalist. He can no more solve all social problems than Christ, The Master, who from time to time fed thousands, more often fed no one. But he cared and he was there. Every committed Christian social reformer must remember that, as the trumpet blows for the final judgment, there will still be at least one major injustice still to be remedied. Heart, courage, and presence, therefore, are more important than schemes. Who has courage to tell a man he must die? Who does him a favor by lying? In Timbuktu, Recife, or the South Bronx, people must be helped to realize that at least for them and now there are no answers. This is the time for friends, perhaps only to hold a hand, to talk about the next life. These are the relationships which keep the poor sane, to say nothing of keeping them Christian.

NOTES FOR CHAPTER SEVEN

1 St. John's University, May 11, 1974.

2 Barbara Ward, *Faith and Freedom,* (New York: W. W. Norton, 1954), p. 265.

3 Quotation of Joseph Vialatoux in Henri Fesquet's *Catholicism: Religion of Tomorrow?,* (New York: Holt, Rinehart and Winston, 1964), p. 174.

4 Ludwig Von Mises, *The Anti-Capitalist Mentality,* (So. Holland, Illinois: Libertarian, 1972); F. A. Hayek, *The Road to Serfdom,* (Chicago:

University of Chicago, 1944); Hilaire Belloc, *The Crisis of Civilization* (New York, Fordham University, 1937).

5 For a late fulmination see John Eppstein, *The Cult of Revolution in the Church*, (New Rochelle, New York: Arlington House, 1974), pp. 140-141. He calls the merger a "vulgar practice" because while the state is a political organ whose function is order, nation (society) is a cultural community with its own heritage and varying religious, language, and intellectual traditions.

6 See Edward J. Kieran, *Arthur J. Penty: His Contribution to Social Thought*, Washington, D. C.: (Catholic University of America, 1941), pp. 137 ff.

7 John Eppstein, *op. cit.*, pp. 41 ff.

8 George G. Higgins, "After Sixty Years," *Catholic Mind*, October, 1951, pp. 610-11.

9 On the importance of personalism as an element in the Catholic social program, see Paul Hanly Furfey, "Personalistic Social Action in 'Rerum Novarum' and 'Quadragesimo Anno' ", *American Catholic Sociological Review*, vol. 2, December 1941, pp. 204-216. Furfey has written a biting piece of social criticism called *The Respectable Murderers* (New York: Herder and Herder, 1966) which drew little attention because it dealt with the failures of people, more than structures.

10 Daniel Bell, *op. cit.*, p. 444.

11 St. John's University, May 11, 1974.

CHAPTER EIGHT

SEEK FIRST THE KINGDOM OF GOD

"St. Vincent de Paul was a pragmatist in the best sense of the word. He saw something to be done and he did it. But the strength and permanence of his approach, which in many ways has revolutionized the apostolate of Charity, resulted from the stress on formation, common sense in structure and organization, but most of all by keeping an eye on God, the beginning and the end, and the sustaining power of prayer. The world has seen little as effective since gospel times."

JOSEPH DIRVIN, C.M.
Author of *Louise de Marillac*
Mrs. Seton

There are many reasons why Christians are interested in the poor. Many of them are wrong reasons. To do the right thing for the wrong reason is better than not to do it at all. St. Vincent de Paul is a good example of a man who took his time learning the right reasons.

Monsieur Vincent may have ended his life as a Frenchman beloved by all but in his early years he was no paradigm of social virtue. If anything, he was a man of his world, ambitious to get ahead and fully aware that the place for a peasant to get ahead in the seventeenth century was the Church. He even looked down on his farmer-father who scrimped to give the boy an education. Once in the priesthood he set his eyes on the episcopacy. Then Dame Fate intervened. He was captured by Turkish pirates and sold into African slavery. It was this captivity which changed his sense of direction. By the time he escaped back to France he was a man of faith, conscious of the presence of God in human affairs, convinced of the foolishness of his worldly ambitions.

That conversion was necessary before the life of Monsieur Vincent, as the father of Catholic Charity, could really begin. His first social cause was the men who manned the Mediterranean galleys, those floating hells so well described by Victor Hugo in *Les Miserables*. He became their visitor, their consoler and defender. He equipped a hospital to which these miserable oarsmen were taken, when sick or laid low by the beatings they took from their masters. Then he reached out to the wretched peasants of France who had been reduced almost to animal life by a succession of rapacious wars. To spread this apostolate he organized the priests of St. Lazarus—now bearing his Vincentian name, many of whom were sent to minister to the enslaved Christians of Northern Africa and to Asia. He took sisters out of their cloisters and brought them into the world, those Daughters of Charity, whose trademark for several centuries were huge flapping gull-wing caps. He changed fashionable and perfumed noblewomen into Ladies of Charity, who later took care of the sick poor and little children literally dropped into gutters by parents who no longer could find them food.

For all the efficiency and method he brought to charity—"Le Bon Monsieur Vincent," as he became known, looked upon himself as a person with "black and boiling moods" and a "dried up, caustic temper." But outsiders saw him at eighty, fastened to his bed, his legs swollen and ulcerous, only able to raise himself by a rope hanging from a hook in the ceiling, repeating his prayers "I am ready," "I believe," "I trust." Robert Leckie, who claims the saints are his heroes, summarizes the secret of men like Vincent de Paul.

> Such belief, such trust, such love proclaim the existence of God. For without God the conduct of these saints is inexplicable. Who else renounces self without denouncing someone else or something?[1]

The world view and life style of this social reforming saint is worth analyzing for the reason that he seems to bear little resemblance to the activists of our day. One wonders how much of the current doings, even by priests and religious, is related to religion. Sometimes, the involvement seems more American than Catholic, well meaning but thoughtless, perhaps best symbolized by the answer of a priest at a CYO boxing contest to a questioning skeptic who, mocking the furious signs of the cross made by one young lad, asked: "Does that stuff help?" "Sure," said the priest, "If he can fight." Then come serious scoffers who ponderously decide that the best way to serve the poor is to leave the Church. In either case, two clearly distinct approaches to the cure of poverty exist side by side. The secularist approach is man-centered; the Christian is by definition God-centered. One proceeds on its own ingenuity; the other depends besides on the mysterious movement of God, the final resting place of all men. The believer associates poverty with more than money, identifies a full stomach as only one human desideratum, and determines human success, not on the last day of living, but on the first day of eternity. The secularist with the narrower world view and the need of final answers enjoys a larger range of immediate choices. He can indulge his angers and his impatience, even if they only console him, with little effect on the lot of the poor.

The likes of Paul VI invite dismay and derision when they say what the Pope said to this-world oriented delegates to the 1974 *World Food Conference* in Rome.

> It is inadmissible that those who have control of the wealth and resources of mankind should try to resolve the problems of hunger by forbidding the poor to be born.[2]

To rational human engineers this Papal statement is an insensible and insane comment. Better to feed one mouth well than two mouths scantily, the sensible argument goes. Common sense suggests that body-care is the important value, and mathematics is the science to determine when the quality of body-care is below standard. Except, the Pope does not accept either that view or that norm.

The story of man's salvation (for a Pope) is recorded in the books which describe God's search for man. The Pope knows that God spoke to man first, before man fully knew who he was. For the man of faith all that is man, all that he has, is God's gift, even his pain and his poverty. The CYO boxer fights as if all depends on his fistic technique, but the sign of the Cross is his public acknowledgment that even this small experience is wrapped up in God's mysterious plan for him. This may also explain why the "Amen" is so frequently louder than the prayer. God sent man the Word in Jesus Christ. That Word ought to be heard. Men ought to think about it and talk about it. Within Christ's family, otherwise named the Church, the struggle every day to survive, to develop, to be enriched as human persons, must be related to that Word. So, the truly Christian apostolate to the poor—while it may look the same as secular works—is not possible "without the hearing of God's word, without the sacraments, without public and private prayer."[3] The ever-present danger for all reformers in the field is the temptation to undervalue the power of the Word. Even if well-intentioned zealots succeed in making the poor man a well-heeled and greedy capitalist, from the vantage point of the Word they have not done him much favor.

To the wise men of this world, this faith-view is foolish. But it still remains an old Catholic message and, in view of the fragility of the newer gospels, one whose time may have come to receive another try. Sometime before the dawn of man's most knowledgeable century, an old Pope, who expected "soon to depart this life, made the argument:

> If human society is to be cured, only a return to Christian life and institutions will cure it.[4]

How many contemporary social reformers really believe that? How many even give thought to the condition of the world in terms of men's morals? Those who maintain that evils cannot be legislated or penalized out of existence are the very ones who would force by law social charity and social justice. In the one instance they favor permissive laws on divorce, abortion, drug use and so-called private morals; but strict laws on tax matters and corporate or government practices. In the lives of individual men, to be sure, there are moral inconsistencies. Men who lead depraved private lives can be scrupulously honest public officials, and vice versa. For this reason there is a general hesitancy to predict the quality of a particular public service from a private record either of regular Church attendance or habits of adultery. However, when the private morals of a nation decline, all the labor unions and welfare legislation in the world are to no avail. If the men who manage those institutions are bad men, no good can be expected in the name of human betterment. The pursuit of private interest, profit and pleasure in the United States has been justified in the name of freedom, so much since World War I that, according to Martha Wolfenstein, we live in the age of "fun morality."[5] Not only the birds and the bees do it, but babies are to be trained for fun-city living. According to Wolfenstein:

> Fun, from having been suspect, has tended to become obligatory. Instead of having too much fun, one is inclined to feel ashamed if one does not have enough.[6]

Words like "virtue," "character," "sin," "self-denial," "penance" are stereotyped on the frozen faces of Ebenezer Scrooge and Carrie Nation, not in the warm but disciplined personalities of Jesus Christ or St. Elizabeth Ann Seton. Existential man is never quite saintly when his principles are noble, and is not necessarily diabolic even when he sells his soul to the devil. But national practices tend to follow culture and culture grows out of accepted ideas. Dishonesty and corruption, brutality and inhumanity, social and sexual deviance, are found in all cultures. In the United States, however, these behavior patterns tend to be highly organized and strongly defended. The evangelists of "fun morality" express horror at the excesses of My Lai, Watergate, Kent State or when rates of abortion, divorce, unemployment, or murder rise to excess. But they would fight to the death any social effort which might limit the supply of call-girls at conventions, or deny ready access to alcohol or contraceptives by teenagers, or elevate the quality of American products or the standards for college admissions. Big business now includes profit-making cultural efforts to keep American moral standards low. The statistics show that the market for these products is widening.

The Church always relates private morals with social witness and community standards. She is one of the few remaining institutions which disqualifies men from ecclesiastical office for moral defects (if they are discovered in time). Pius XI, one of the most pragmatic churchmen of this century, based his plan for the reconstruction of the social order on a reform of institutions which went hand in hand with a reform of morals. Were this mountain-climber around today, he would tell a generation, which equates tinkering with structures with a certain guarantee of justice, that their efforts, if not "preceded by a renewal of the Christian spirit," are wasted.[7] This may be the hardest task of all, which is why secular society shuns the labor. And harder still because the Church which defines sin in terms of acts against God, neighbor, self and society in that order, now has theologians saying that the special evil of sin is not so much in the deed but in its social consequences. Since the long-range results of people's sinning are hidden from them, when they take a little graft, raise a wage or price a little, do only a little fornicating, it is no wonder that sins are on the increase.

To cite a single example, Christians might cure inflation and moderate the appetites of a consumer-sated society, if they developed a spirit of poverty or detachment in their own lives. Part of our problem is that we, like Michael Harrington in *The Other America,* call ourselves poor whenever we live below the standard to which we have become accustomed. Harrington said there were fifty million poor. But the number might be double that if people were asked to locate themselves. Even those forced to take off weight to become healthy would then be represented in poverty groups. Or, if Christians could really acquire charity, governments would not be tempted to invent compulsory machinery to equalize groups. Equality in rights is the natural order of things, as Adolph Hitler was once reminded:

as God's sun shines on all that bear human countenance, so does His Law know no privileges or exceptions.[8]

The non-violent pacifism of Christians should not need engineering and the world might be a better place to live in, if sociologists realized that "the forces that are to renew the face of the Earth should proceed from within."[9]

Those embarking on the mission of social reconstruction for the Catholic community ought to steep themselves in the relevant folklore of their own tradition. The principles governing the approach of St. Vincent de Paul are standardly Catholic and quite appropriate for study by those to whom he is no more than a name.

The basic element of Vincent's apostolate to the poor was the search for the will of God and the mind of Jesus Christ.[10] For the follower of Him whose departing words included "Not my will but thine be done," this is common doctrine. What sometimes goes on in the name of social reform is hardly related to any discernible will of God. When Vincent was engaged in designing the apostolate of the Daughters of Charity, he told them:

> To be true Daughters of Charity you must do what the Son of God did when He was on Earth. And what did He chiefly do? After submitting His will, by obeying the Blessed Virgin and St. Joseph, He labored unceasingly for His neighbor, visiting and healing the sick and instructing the ignorant unto their salvation.[11]

Joseph Dirvin calls Vincent a "Christian Existentialist," i.e., the man who moved to do the practical thing, once he was convinced that God willed that such and such must be done here and now. In fact he would hold back projects until the signs of God's Providence were in evidence. Even his most lasting, and likely his greatest works, the establishment of the Priests of the Mission and the Daughters of Charity, was not the result of any special preference of his own. Once in explaining the rules of the community to his priests, he is recorded on May 17, 1658 as making this somber comment:

> O Savior! Such Rules! And where did they come from? Did I think of them? Not at all, gentlemen, for I never had a

thought either of rule or of the company or even of the word mission. God did all that.

According to Dirvin he found the will of God in two sources: (1) The directives and requests of bishops, spiritual directors, patrons, etc., (2) The most urgent needs of the Church, urgent need being defined as that about which no one else bothered. His second sign of divine pleasure would still be generally accepted as a good norm for today, but his first would encounter bluster and denial from those who would broaden the base of the Church to include more than leadership. Yet, in the history of Christian spirituality the special charisms of office, as well as people, have in fact been quite salvific. If not everything a superior person does can be related by chain reaction back to God, there is still value in the concept that the "official" decision, presuming it is seriously made, requires respect and compliance, and becomes the will of God for someone.

Even the idea of establishing the Vincentian Fathers is not claimed by the founder at all. A certain Madame de Gondi started him off by asking Vincent to arrange periodic missions for those residing on her estates. As her chaplain, he tried to accommodate her by obtaining religious orders of Paris for the project. They were not interested. Undaunted, the willfull lady importuned her brother-in-law, the Archbishop of Paris, to encourage Vincent himself to establish a community of missionaries. Vincent took the request as a sign of God's will. Later it required the Archbishop's intervention before he would permit the Daughters of Charity to work in the celebrated Parisian hospital, the Hotel Dieu. The evangelization of countryside French peasants was thrust upon him by the awareness that almost everyone else in the Church seemed to have abandoned them.

Thinking such as this is directly at odds with the prevailing mood of some contemporary religious congregations. The notion, for example, that spiritual formation must precede apostolic work is being abandoned in favor of a policy which equates doing good works with religious formation. One religious community has for four years refused to acknowledge directives of the Holy See which call for an end to practices which denigrate the supernatural aspects of apostolic work.[12] Words like "supernatural" have been removed from the theology of some congregations. The stress on purely secular works is so assertive that some new constitutions of religious congregations read more like documents put out by the public relations office of a large corporation. Questions about personal union with God seem no longer to be asked. This represents a radical break with Catholic tradition. The Church's salvific mission to "build up the body of Christ," "to save souls," "to lead mankind" to the New Jerusalem is scarcely mentioned, while the promotion of the social and political improvement of men has become the preferred calling.

St. Vincent de Paul would have none of this. His first interest was God's grand design. When Louise de Marillac pressed for the establishment of a religious community of nuns, he told her firmly:

> I beseech you, once and for all, not to think about it until Our Lord shows that it is His will, and at present the sentiments which He inspires are quite to the contrary.[13]

On another occasion he bade her to seek the guidance of her bishop:

> Offer to retrench any part of your procedure, if he so pleases, and to quit it entirely if that is what he wants. Such is the spirit of God. I find no blessing except in acting thus. Msgr. de Chalon is a holy man. You ought to regard him as the interpreter of the will of God.[14]

He constantly warned his own confreres of the snares and delusions waiting for them and of how the good works of God will be misread even by the elect. On December 6, 1658 he told them:

> There will come a day when mischievous spirits will decry the good works God had led us to embrace and hold in benediction. I warn the Company of it so that it will look at things as they are, as the works of God, which God confided to us without our

having injected ourselves into a single one nor contributed in any way to drawing attention to ourselves. They have been confided to us either by those empowered to do so or by pure necessity, which are the paths by which God led us into these designs.[15]

Admittedly, the search for God's will is not always easy and differs in mode from culture to culture. Those with responsible positions for the care of the faithful vary in their perception of need, and "pure necessity thrust upon us" provides the latitude for the creative Christian interested in reading the expressions of God's design. However, the enduring value of Vincent's leadership is found in the declaration, time and time again and in varying ways, that spirituality is to be measured in inverse proportion to the amount of self contained in the answer to a question. Father Dirvin considers these spiritual principles not only "humanitarian" but "liberating" and ones to be ignored at one's own peril.

I have seen too often dedicated priests, nuns, and laity plunge into the ghettos of spiritual and temporal misery, so completely and absorbedly, that horrified by the inhumanity and injustice they encountered that, forgetting the safeguards of prayer and rule, they disappeared, swallowed up by the very horror they had come to conquer.[16]

St. Vincent would have been deeply disturbed by sentiments such as the following which seem to lack a spiritual dimension, and even fair judgment:

The priest has traditionally been the obedient and docile functionary of an authoritarian system. He had little room for initiative that was foreign to the will of the bishop, and less room for independence. Generations of priests endured the repressions and restraints that were part and parcel of that mode of existence, but today's priest will not. He insists on freedom and responsibility commensurate with adulthood, education, and office, and he is willing to battle publicly for them.[17]

Apart from the questionable presumption of magazines such as *Commonweal*, whose view of the Church is frequently colored by priests, whose frustrations are always of Homeric proportions, the concept of the rebel priest, nun, apostolic lay worker has no place in Vincentian theology or in spiritual exercises. If the priests whose social apostolate was frustrated by bishops were laid end to end, it is just possible that the books about frustrations would outnumber the books about apostolic works. Bishops in Vincent's time may have supervised priests closely and might have been called stiflers of initiative. But the spectre of American bishops waving their crozier around a diocese hooking energetic priests into immobility and lassitude is nothing more than a contrived and fabricated distortion of isolated fact. The general truth is that in the contemporary Church almost no bishop has interfered with anyone's particular response to the Vincentian "pure necessity." Religious assignments, to be sure, do limit their activity to a minor proportion of the week's hours. But in the American priesthood almost everyone has been free to engage in his own avocation, with no one around to direct, supervise, or coordinate what he was doing. This vacuum in itself has been a critical defect in what supposedly is a well-functioning system. Another fact worth remembering is that most of the good things done for the poor by Catholics have been done in collaboration with bishops. Social activists may without fault complain they did not receive encouragement, promotion or financial backing to their satisfaction. The complaint of episcopal interference and oppression is quite different. But even in the isolated case where a bishop gives a direct order to a priest, the Vincentian counsel to the priest seems obvious.

The French father of Catholic charity, for all his compassion and Christian love, was never dominated by the modern affliction called sentimentality. For power to destroy the meaning of charity and the human person, he would consider the sentimentalist a dangerous person. G. K. Chesterton's definition of the sentimentalist as a man who "seeks to enjoy every idea without its sequence, and every pleasure without its consequence" would have met Vincent's approval. The very nature of his spiritual view of poverty prevented him from becoming a little god who determined what is right for everybody. Nor would he have become so saturated by his own tears shed over the misfortunes of the few, that he would trample the rights of majorities. The natural consequence of sentimentalism is the denial to the poor of the right to have babies and abortion for those happenstancely conceived.

One biography sums up Vincent's approach to his Lords the poor, as he called them:

> A wave of compassion was just beginning to sweep over France, bringing with it an awakening to the terrible lot of many of the peasantry, ground down, as they were, by merciless taxation. Deaths from cold, hunger, or neglect were ordinary events. Vincent, already aware of these conditions, became even more so as he travelled over one district after another of Northern France. Yet he, practical peasant that he was, refused to be carried away by them. He eyed them with sympathy, yet with shrewdness too, and incidents which would have doubtless shocked the town-dweller, left him questioning. Genuine misery he was ready to alleviate at any price, but for the professional beggar, or those eager to make parade of their afflictions, he had small sympathy.[18]

If Vincent found a man, for whom he had procured work, once again in the soup line at St. Lazare, he sent him packing. In the coffers of Vincent's charity, there was no subsidy for wilful idleness.

Because working for the poor is both difficult and dangerous he did not see how God's will could be done unless they themselves were spiritually qualified. His disciple Louise de Marillac made the same point to her nuns.

> Those called by God to his holy work ought on the one hand try to render themselves worthy by the practicing of the virtues required for it and by the exact observance of their rules, and on the other to excite themselves and to possess great confidence in our Lord Jesus Christ . . . (because it is a service

done) to His own Person, and consequently He will not fail to supply in return the graces necessary to surmount all difficulties they might encounter in it, to say nothing of the rich crown reserved for them in heaven.[19]

This pithy compendium of the requirements of a Christian social apostolate prompted Joseph Dirvin to list four basic rules for servants to the poor.

First, because it is too dangerous to assume on one's own, the minister of the poor must be called to it by God. Secondly, he must make himself worthy of the calling by the practice of virtue and a deep prayer life. Thirdly, he must serve the poor and the miserable because he truly sees Christ in them, not because he is engaged in a sociological exercise. Fourthly, he has complete confidence in God and a humble appreciation of his own expertise.[20]

In other words engagement in the problems of the poor—at least from a Catholic point of view—was not a work for spiritual lightweights. Compassion was necessary but only when combined with discipline. Vincent may have been a benevolent teacher but he was also a single-minded director. His age, like our own, was a mixture of the softness and slackness associated with the Bourbon throne and the Jansenist hardness of Port-Royal's nuns. Vincent reacted with horror at both these excesses. C. C. Martindale recaps the balance of his program.

Half-measures were intolerable in those who had given their lives to God's direct service. Hence his letters are as austere as they are affectionate, shrewd, levelheaded, vivacious. Thus, in our age of selfishness, we have an example of absolute, self-sacrificing love; in our age of sentimentalism, we have an example of rigid adherence to principle, and to an exacting ideal. Christ asks lovingly from his Christians, but he asks much.[21]

Seldom is there mention in recent years about the strictures imposed by Christian tradition on those who would become social apostles for Christ's sake. The respective mottos of his religious communities—*Evangelizare pauperibus misit me* for the confreres, *Caritas Christi urget nos* for the daughters, linked the inseparable elements of the Christian charism for the poor: preach the gospel to the poor while tending to their bodily and psychic needs. It may be true that the man with the empty stomach is not likely disposed to preachment, but the preacher is interested in far more than merely filling a belly. There is one Vincentian aphorism relevant to a secular age. Give the sacraments to the poor before anything else.

The Catholic approach to the poor has its own wholeness. Those engaged in only one of its segments—dispensing soup in a public kitchen or arbitrating a labor dispute—must understand the incompleteness of their labor. That is why the Church wants its apostolic laborers constantly reminded of the totality of life. Pius XI in *Quadragesimo Anno* even had a prescription for Catholic leaders of trade unions.

> Side by side with these (neutral) unions there should always be associations zealously engaged in imbuing and forming their members in the teaching of religion and morality so that they in turn may be able to permeate the unions with that good spirit which should direct all their activity.[22]

Anyone acting in the name of the Christian community is engaged primarily in building up the Kingdom of God on Earth. Works of justice and mercy are service instruments but also means of bringing men to Christ. By these works people must know about Christ and redemption. Those immersed in the physical distress of the poor sometimes become embarrassed about its religious dimension. If so, they need to re-examine their own motives and qualifications. Catholics sometimes known as social reformers are not evangelists because their intentions exclude preaching the gospel. The Christian process of filling bellies ought to contain at least a reminder concerning the source of the manna.

The man of faith is a different advocate of the poor man's

cause, whether he be on a picket line, in the legislature, or in chapel. At a given moment he may be doing what the poor man wants or doing something else entirely. He may be walking in step with the latest political action program, an approved member of backroom caucuses, and his name may receive favorable mention by the press. On the other hand, the Catholic social actionist may be a Jeremiah, who confronts blind leaders of the blind because he is interested in long-range betterment, not short-range huckstering. He may find himself leading crusades or playing the role of great reconciler. His problems may include people on welfare lines who stand three days in line without assistance, the sick whose pains make medicaid-doctors richer, men unable to find employment, or welfare chiselers, professional mendicants, and life-time loafers. There is the support of legitimate wage demands and opposition to trade union extortion, condemnation of exorbitant profits and defense of the freedom to own, friendship with socially-minded legislators and hostility to statists. The advocate of Christian social reform must be able to decide where he stands and his positions are not always predictable.

No two ages or nations are the same. Those committed to the Christian world view must learn how to apply those values in a non-discriminatory way. American bishops used to quote the papal encyclicals in favor of the socialized use of private property, while Polish bishops simultaneously sitting under the Soviet gun were quoting the same encyclicals against unreasonable restrictions on private ownership. In America, what William Whyte calls the "social ethic" came about as a response to a system of individual enterprise motivated by the survival of the fittest under which millions were hurt. In Poland it was the excesses of governmentalization that needed remedy through allowable individual enterprise.

No responsible Christian, conscious of the social gospel, rejects the growth of Big Business, Big Labor, Big Government or denies their contributions to general being. These collectivities may not have turned the welfare state into a Garden of Eden, but neither have they made hell for man on earth, as some modern medievalists suggest. But there are new problems. Whyte raises questions which have not been fairly answered: Are Big Business, Big Labor, and Big Government now tending to work against people's well-being? Are they any longer the only answers? If not, what are some alternatives? Whyte offers an answer of his own.

> Precisely because it is an age of organization, it is the other side of the coin that needs emphasis. We do need to know how to cooperate with the Organization, but, more than ever, so do we need to know how to resist it. Out of context this would be an irresponsible statement. Time and place are critical, and history has taught us that a philosophical individualism can venerate conflict too much and cooperation too little. But what is the context today? The tide has swung far enough the other way. I submit that we need not worry that a counter emphasis will stimulate people to an excess of individualism.[23]

The emotional detachment of the Christian, therefore, is important. How does a Christian fight the system? Does he fight destructively? Does he tell everyone to go to hell, go his own way, and leave the system intact? Does he succumb to the system, or make a nuisance of himself, or work for changes, or move to some private tropic isle? Radicals, especially the violent ones, experience a therapeutic kick from nonconformity. Their lasting contribution to the therapy of a sick society seems small. Whyte thinks the successful game is won by those with "know how." Lyndon Johnson's "know how" of the legislative process meant more to the long-range well-being of the Black man than all the bluster and campuus riots of his presidency. His signed bills which endorsed and guaranteed equality in public accommodations, in jobs and in voting are the keys which will unlock doors to the Black for generations to come.

Detachment from vested interests is a more difficult virtue for social apostles to acquire. Some promoters lose their ardor for poor causes when they become part of the cursed system. Some live lush lives on money intended more for the poor than for middlemen. Agitators of the poor become more obstreperous because they fail to make it with the system. The Christian advocate

will always have a fight on his hands to remain above the corrupting influence of secular partisans. Spirit, judgment and patience and charity are the virtues which count. St Vincent de Paul
fought a king over the enforced jailing of 80,000 beggars because
mass incarceration was inhuman. Yet, he considered many of those
beggars despicable because in their pursuit of a dishonest sou they
used foundlings to gain them sympathy from alms-givers. St. Vincent de Paul was the captive neither of kings nor beggars, only of
Christ.

NOTES FOR CHAPTER EIGHT

1 Robert Leckie, *These Are My Heroes,* (New York: Random House,
1964), p. 11.

2 *New York Times,* November 10, 1974, p. 1.

3 Max De Lespesse, *The Church Community: Leaven and Life Style,*
(Notre Dame, Indiana: Ave Maria, 1973), p. 49.

4 Leo XIII, *Rerum Novarum,* May 15, 1891.

5 Martha Wolfenstein, "Fun Morality: An Analysis of Recent American
Child-Training Literature" in Margaret Mead and Martha Wolfenstein
(eds.), *Childhood in Contemporary Cultures,* (Chicago: University of Chicago, 1955), pp. 168-174.

6 *Ibid,* p. 168.

7 Pius XI, *Quadragesimo Anno,* May 15, 1931.

8 Pius XI, *Mit Brenender Sorge,* 1936.

9 Pius XII, *Summi Pontificatus,* 1939.

10 Most of the commentary to follow is drawn from an unpublished
statement of Joseph Dirvin, C.M. entitled "The Vincentian Apostolate to the
Poor," presented at St. John's University, May 13, 1973.

11 *Conferences,* vol. 1, pp. 13-14; Dirvin—Lidem, p. 117.

12 *National Catholic Reporter,* February 12, 1971, p. 1. The headline
reads: "Sisters Want to Drop Renewal."

13 Quoted by Joseph Dirvin from *Letters of St. Vincent de Paul,* selected
and edited by Joseph Leonard, C.M. (Paris, Archives of the Congregation of
the Mission), p. 63.

14 *Ibid.,* pp. 136-137.

15 Quoted by Joseph Dirvin from Joseph Leonard, C.M., *The Conferences of St. Vincent de Paul to the Sisters of Charity,* (Westminster, Maryland: Newman, 1952), conference dated December 6, 1658.

16 St. John's University, May 13, 1974.

17 Editorial, "The Priest as Rebel," in *Commonweal,* October 6, 1967, p. 6.

18 M. V. Woodgate, *Saint Vincent de Paul,* (Westminster, Maryland, 1960), p. 23.

19 St. Louise de Marillac, "Regles Pour Les Filles de La Charite Qui Sont Soin Des Galeriens, Pouvant Servir A Toutes Sortes De Prisons" in her *Correspondence, Meditations, Pensees, Avis,* (Paris, 1961), pp. 991-992.

20 St. John's University, May 11, 1973.

21 C. C. Martindale, S.J., *St. Vincent de Paul,* (London: Catholic Truth Society, 1959), pp. 31-32.

22 No. 35.

23 William H. Whyte, Jr., *The Organization Man,* (New York: Simon and Schuster, 1956), p. 14.

CHAPTER NINE

THE QUESTIONS PEOPLE ASK?

"I am a member of the United Methodist Church. We have many of the problems of the Roman Catholic Church. If the Church, yours or mine, is to be the community of those who love in the service of those who need, then it must broaden its base. Our mission is to share hearts and pocketbooks, not only with those who belong to us but with those who are not part of our fellowship and are far poorer than we."

Rev. Calvin Pressley, Director
Opportunities Industrialization
Center of New York Inc.

About the Condition of the Poor

Are not some of these"so-called" poor people earning good money?

Msgr. John Ahern: If you walk into a nursing home or a hospital looking for the barest employment, they will put a mop in your hand for $172 a week. That comes to $8,944 a year. These are heads of families I am talking about. Off the top come income taxes, Social Security taxes and carfare. The real take-home pay is about $120 per week. That is not much to shelter, feed and clothe a family today.

* * * * *

How poor are the poor in other sections of the country beside the East and the West?

Sr. Grace Foley: Rural Virginia, where I am assigned, houses one-third of the state's population. But in this area two-thirds of the homes have no plumbing. As you might expect they are also dilapidated and overcrowded. In the Shenandoah Valley 24 percent of the rural houses lack toilets, 29 percent lack piped water. In one small mountainside town (population less than 5,000) there are 830 families earning less than $3,000. In the rural South one does not talk of a poverty level cut-off of $4,000, because in many instances people are existing on half that amount. Appalachia, which is 92 percent White, has nine of ten of its families living in dire poverty.

* * * * *

Why is so little said about the psychological handicaps of poverty?

Nicholas Kisburg: Psychological handicaps more frequently arise out of the culture than mere lack of money. I know welfare families with two television sets, and working families that have none. I could afford ten television sets but have only one. But in our society which penalizes failure, a father is often nothing to his children unless he can provide two television sets, and at least one automobile. Many psychological problems are society made.

One frustration of the poor is the result of their inability to get service. If he complains to the city about no hot water, no painting, the complaint will be put on the bottom of a pile. On the other hand, my landlord is scared to death of me. I call him and he knows I will go to the headman of the housing department, so my house is painted the next day.

Or consider the language problem. Just think what happens to the Spanish pride of a Puerto Rican man who has to take his complaint down to City Hall only to find no one understands that he has a legitimate problem. In fairness, the municipal bureaucrat who feels harassed at the moment, is annoyed enough to complain: "Why doesn't this man learn to speak English? I did. I was poor." Kenneth Clark maintained, and he was right, the White middle class teacher will never relate psychologically to the poor Black in the ghetto. The language barrier explains the difficulties between the poor and the police.

The inability to cope with the environment around you can be devastating. The previous poor were even poorer than the Blacks and Puerto Ricans today, but capitalism was expanding, and if they worked hard most of them could make it.

I also think we got rid of poverty with the Irish, Italians and Jews by killing half of them off with high death rates. But now a man can work 2,000 hours a year and still be in poverty. There is a terrible sense around that "I am not master of my destiny. I cannot control things." If I feel that way, can you imagine how the man at the bottom feels?

*　*　*　*　*

The fact that a neophyte street cleaner can earn more than an experienced bank clerk, is not that one of our psychological problems?

Fr. Philip Carey: Yes but labor unions are not to blame for that. The entire American economy runs on catching up with someone else's more. Why does General Motors advertise? To make people dissatisfied with last year's model. Unions move up on each other to catch up with last year's prices. And what some workers do not get from collective bargaining, others get through political action or even by the largesse of employers.

*　*　*　*　*

Why is the economics of this question so important?

Mr. Walter Hooke: Not as important as it is made out to be. Years ago moving hourly rates from 25 to 30 cents, weekly wages from $16 to $18 brought the cry of bankruptcy. There just is no precise bottom line for wages. If a decent wage was paid, the price would always be high enough for the efficient grower to make a dollar and low enough for the consumer to have his Caesar's salad.

*　*　*　*　*

What about some responsibility among the poor? It is a delusion to believe that alcoholics, drug addicts, loafers have not the ability to help themselves. Not all people's problems are created by other people. Groups like Alcoholics Anonymous and Daytop are constantly reminding members to stop kidding themselves and grow up to some maturity.

Dolores Huerta: Everybody has to take responsibility, including the poor. Even going on strike is an exercise in responsibility. We do not let our members shift responsibility to anyone else. The responsible union leader makes sure that no one cops out. If the man in question is an alcoholic he is told "If you want to stay with us you go get a cure." A poor man is not a saint. He has his faults to be treated as you would treat one of your own family, and that includes consideration and affection, but it also includes making him carry his share of responsibility.

* * * * *

ABOUT THE UNITED STATES

Is not the fact that some wages have gone up drastically in a short time a reason for our inflation?

Mr. Nicholas Kisburg: Wages are a considerable portion of total costs, probably 70 percent. But there are two things to consider. First, inequality of levels of improvement. Do not ask, however, why the truck driver gets more than the teachers, but why is it fair for the teacher to get less than the truck driver? Secondly, the question of depressed wages. If you exploit hospital workers long enough, at rates under two dollars an hour for example, a revolution is in the offing. Had justice been done in the first place, the wage increases would have been painless.

I agree that some wage increases came too fast. But from the worker's viewpoint wages are not absolutes but relative. It is not so much a factor that the hospital orderly went from two to three dollars, but the nurse's aide who had three now wants four, and the elevator operator at four wants five and so on. It is not so much the money which gives status, as the differential with the group below. And because these differentials are necessary, American society is just going to have to live with them.

But even admitting the importance of wages, I must say that other things are more important. Most conservative economists agree unions had nothing to do with the latest inflation. Government spending, the money supply, and the prime interest rate are more important to this inflation. When the Government pours money into the economy which it must borrow, and the Federal Reserve Board releases the cash, and the First National City raises the prime interest rate to 12 percent, prices are going up, and the increase in the minimum wage from $1.60 to $2.00 had little to do with that rise.

* * * * *

Is government more responsive today?

Mr. Nicholas Kisburg: Yes much more than forty, thirty, or twenty years ago. But, and this is a big but, the more responsive the government, the more frustrated the people. Why? The revolution of rising expectations. That is why. The bottom line of expectation for everyone is that television, that automobile, that everything. But not everyone can have everything and man is not likely to solve either the problem of getting everything he wants or of satisfying his ego needs when he fails to get everything.

* * * * *

ABOUT THE UNITED STATES

The American people represent six percent of the world's family but consume forty percent of the world's goods. What would it mean to a Third World person with his level of living to hear that an American cannot live on $10,000 a year?

Nicholas Kisburg: The answer has nothing to do with the $10,000 figure. A welfare family of four in New York City has a higher standard of living than the average unskilled workingman in Great Britain. An English worker with an annual income of $10,000 would live like a proverbial millionaire. As a matter of fact, many naturalized citizens return to their old country to live well by camparison with natives on their company union pension plus Social Security. Americans are especially blessed. The problem is not their productivity or good fortune but the inability to develop mechanisms of equal productivity elsewhere. But even then the American standard would create envy. The problems of poor people are not going to be solved by taking from the rich. Ask the Russians.

*　*　*　*　*

What are some political obstacles to the international redistribution of wealth?

Msgr. George Higgins: The American political situation, for one. Even presuming that our economy has 10 billion dollars—make it 25 if you will—to redistribute, it is not likely that the American people are going to elect the kind of Congress which will give that away in foreign aid. The American poor will be among the most reluctant. Citizens can be steamed up about the domestic economy, but Congressmen report that they receive little pressure about money bills for foreign countries from anyone, religious as well as millionaires.

*　*　*　*　*

How is it that legislators, even those who vote right on the right issues, may not be really responsive to the people who elected them?

Congressman Carey: Because the people who elected them have no machinery to rate the efficiency of the legislator in terms of their political needs. And lacking that, they are unable to call him to account. National lobbying organizations like COPE draw up a score card of key issues, National Health Insurance, the new minimum wage, the housing bill and pass out marks. By those standards some politicians get failing marks, the world is told about it, and their constituents are urged to get these failures out of office. Legislators respond to that kind of pressure.

Unorganized voters, particularly at the community level, at present have no such political power: Take, for example, what happened as a result of the *Supplementary Security Insurance* program. The government decided that the aged, the blind and the disabled would be served better with a supplemented social security program administered by the federal government, than by one administered by local welfare departments. In actual fact, the new program gave senior and handicapped citizens less money than the older arrangement. Here is where local political action groups ought to come in. They bring the injustice to the attention of the politician, ask what he is going to do about it, demand a monthly report of progress. Politicians find a way of helping each other if "no progress" on some important issue may cause a friend to lose his seat in the legislature.

I do not know anyone who rates legislators on their response to the community. Local political action offices are the answer. There are instances where councilmen, assemblymen, congressmen serving the same constituency do not speak to each other. The amount of time spent on the floor of Congress listening to someone else's speeches is not so important as how a man spends his time getting the bureaucracy to serve his people.

* * * * *

Does not the Social Security System lock the aged into poverty?

Congressman Carey: The *Social Security System* was and is intended as a supplement to, not the foundation of, an older person's normal income. Social security payments are not set at a sufficiency level. *The Older Americans Act* provides community meals for the aged, much the same as is currently provided for school children.

The regulation governing the earnings of people after 65 years should be re-examined. We place a penalty on the working aged and give employers an unearned dividend. The employer may take a retired accountant, who earned $20,000 last year, work him five days a week for less than $3,200 a year. Otherwise, the retiree must give up his Social Security earnings. Originally, the theory behind payment limits on the elderly was that they would be forced to stay out of competition with younger people looking for work. But in an inflationary economy they are being penalized.

Housing is particularly acute for the elderly who are pressed by rising costs and by landlords who would make more money from their removal. Connecticut frees the elderly from real estate taxes up to an income of $7,500. In New York the limit for such tax relief is only $6,500. The federal tax system penalizes elderly people who file jointly. There are on record cases of elderly people divorcing, living together in common law status, filing separately, to acquire a net gain. The sin is in the tax system, not the people.

* * * * *

ABOUT SOCIAL ACTIVISM

Why should city people be concerned about people thousands of miles away when they have so many of their own problems in front of them?

Mrs. Dolores Huerta: In the case of farm workers the answer is very simple: everyone eats and it is the farmer who puts the food on the table of Mr. Everyman. Everyone profits from the farmer's work and some grow fat because of it. But if adding to the happiness of everyone the farmer finds himself exploited and miserable, who must assume responsibility? Certainly the eaters have some responsibility.

Every box of lettuce ends up in a city store exactly as packaged, even if in a field where there is no drinking water, no place to wash hands, no toilet. Boxes of lettuce do not go through a middleman. So the eater for his own safety has a direct connection with the farm worker.

We cannot expect to help people who are poor unless the more affluent are bothered and made uncomfortable. We can talk about justice and righteousness all we want but unless the poor have strength and the affluent are willing to help, there will be talk, nothing more.

How can the middle class help the poor?

Mrs. Dolores Huerta: First, they can take their place on the picket line. Not everyone can. But those who do help educate the middle class who often are afraid of the poor. Very frequently middle class people in the suburbs do not really know what is going on. They find it hard to believe that policemen peddle dope in the ghetto, although poor parents live with that fact daily. Secondly, once they overcome their own built-in prejudices against Brown and Black people, they can take their new insights and feelings into their churches, schools and community organizations and continue the re-education of the middle class.

*   *   *   *   *

Why do not the new poor do what the old European immigrants did? Save up.

Mrs. Dolores Huerta: Politics and racism make it difficult for the new poor. Take the case of the Chicanos. My grandfather had a farm in New Mexico. The father of Cesar Chavez had a farm in Arizona. Neither of these families have farms any more because they were taken from us. The *Oriental Exclusion Act,* for example, prevented Filipinos from marrying White women and prevented Chinese and Japanese from owning land. Land grabbers and large corporations, even to this day, with almost entirely White ownership, are putting an end to little farms and little growers. If a barber wants to own his own barbershop, this is approved as progress. But in the South and Far West efforts of farm workers to advance themselves, let alone own land, are associated with Communism. Good racism becomes the going political game.

ABOUT TRADE UNIONISM

What is the difference between business and social trade unionism?

Mr. Nicholas Kisburg: Simply the difference between bread and butter issues and social causes. Once I have the boss organized on basics, I want him in business because we are now partners. I might want to debilitate him prior to the contract, if he was offering terms no good for my people. But once I have a contract, I want discipline and order. Put it another way. I might strike for another paid holiday, any additional day, Martin Luther King's birthday, or Adolph Hitler's. It makes no difference as long as it is a day my men get paid for not working. That is business unionism. But every time the *International Longshoremen's Association* decides not to load Russian ships for political, not economic reasons, 3,800 of my truck drivers are out of work. Once the motive is other than economic there is trouble for unionism. Because besides politics, there are morals, social customs, vendettas and just plain gangsterism. Using economic force to promote social causes is the function of other organizations, not trade unions.

*   *   *   *

What are some of the practical difficulties faced by young unions?

Msgr. George Higgins: Places make a difference. Among other things the police force in the valleys of a state like California is entirely different from what we find in the City of New York. New York police may not be notoriously pro-union but would never be allowed to do what police do to strikers in California. Five thousand strikers were jailed last summer in one small county. If the New York police tried to arrest 5,000 Teamsters there would be a revolution. At the least City Hall would be blown up.

Timing also makes a difference. The Teamsters have had the canneries for forty years but did not organize the farm workers. It took someone with a different vision like Cesar Chavez and the right time to succeed. Now there is a new timing. After a five year boycott and a lot of suffering, the Teamsters think this is the time for them to move in.

* * * * *

ABOUT TRADE UNIONISM

To what extent is the self-interest of major trade unions fueling up inflation which is murder for people on the bottom? Should we really be thinking of a wage system which has a ceiling along with a minimum?

Msgr. George Higgins: If one is going to think along those lines, he better think of prices. As long as an automobile company can unilaterally slap a $125 increase on a new model, which workers are to buy, no union will accept wage restraints only. Theoretically, there would be no difficulty with an economic system which relates wages to prices. A union leader is not going to be any more civic-minded than a businessman.

* * * * *

Is there any good reason for preferring a boycott to a strike?

Msgr. George Higgins: Among other things you cannot put a picket line around a farm that runs for forty miles. In the entire history of the agricultural industry there has never been a successful strike. On the contrary, when the situation involves trucks, there is seldom an unsuccessful strike of Teamsters. Everything depends on control. Farms cannot be controlled like trucks. Hence the importance of the boycott.

Take another example. The Farah Workers in Texas were approached by one of the oldest established unions in the country—the Amalgamated Clothing Workers. This respectable union could get nowhere. The existing N.L.R.B. arrangements, court delays, anti-union newspapers and media, political pressure in El Paso and San Antonio were so hostile the strongest old-line union resorted to what everyone thought had gone out of fashion—the boycott.

* * * * *

What do unions of poor workers do besides raise income for their members?

Mrs. Dolores Huerta : In the past three years we set up a medical program for farm workers, paid for by the growers at the rate of ten cents an hour. We have five clinics, four in California, one in Mexicali for workers who come across the border. A farm worker can get a full medical examination for three dollars, his wife can deliver her baby in one of four clinics for $35, and the families of farm workers are entitled to hospitalization, medical and dental care, X-rays. We have service centers to help them with their immigration problems and a retirement program. What contemporaries are inclined to forget is that Filipino workers were frequently brought in to this country in their teens, were denied the opportunity to bring in wives (so that they could be worked more efficiently) and later denied the right to marry Whites. Many of these bachelors are now senior citizens with no one to care for them. So retirement villages, paid for by a two cent assessment on every box of grapes, are vital.

We also have a credit union which dispensed as loans $2 million and pays a 4½ percent dividend to the investing workers. They borrow their own money at a low rate of interest from a credit union which is managed by people who never went to college. Poor people have brains, too, and the human resources to make such progress work.

* * * * *

Why did the Farm Workers lose all those contracts to the Teamsters?

Mrs. Dolores Huerta: The reason we lost all of the contracts in grapes was because the farm workers had another mission to do.

God works his will in many ways and what looks like a setback sometimes is just another God-given opportunity. Perhaps we lost those contracts so that we would have time to move around the country talking to people. Perhaps because only in a crisis such as this would bishops publicly support our cause and our boycott. Perhaps, too, in order to get more people, including clergy, involved in the cause of the poor and for the right reasons. Supermarket chains are finding their equanimity upset by the presence of what they call "the God-Squad." Our first boycott involved mainly students. Because of our recent troubles the latest boycott has involved clergy.

Losing contracts has stimulated a real spiritual crusade among our members. We have the Virgin of Guadalupe out there on the street and nightly rosaries and fasting on behalf of our cause. When we ask people not to eat lettuce or grapes we are really asking them to join us in a partial fast as atonement for what has been done to our poor.

* * * * *

How come Cesar Chavez lost most of his contracts so that his membership has gone from 60,000 to 4,000?

Msgr. George Higgins: The Teamsters took them. When the contracts expired in grapes, the Teamsters took all but one of them and the people too. But this does not mean that Chavez does not have the members. When the Teamsters took the first lettuce contract, they did not have a single member. They got the growers in a hotel room, presented them with a blank piece of mimeograph paper, and told the growers "sign here." The Teamsters up to that moment had no union meetings. The United Farm Workers have meetings around the clock with one, two, and three thousand in attendance. That means members.

* * * * *

I thought the day of atrocities in dealing with organization efforts was long since past.

7

Mrs. Dolores Huerta: How do you define atrocity? Last year in Southern California a bus owned by one of the growers missed a curve and fell into a large irrigation ditch drowning nineteen of the thirty-seven migrant workers being transported to their jobs. Four of these were women, four came from one family, and one was a thirteen-year-old child. Why did this happen? Because the seats of the bus were not fastened to the floor. In the melee people were crushed one against the other, and those on the bottom of the pile doomed to a watery death. That vehicle should have been banned from the highways as unsafe. But the grower says he is not at fault because that is the responsibility of the labor contractor. The labor contractor's son, by the way, drove the second bus around the accident without so much as looking at the terror going on. I say this is atrocity. And do you know how the labor contractor was penalized for the death of all those farm workers. He was fined $50.

Or take the case of the wine company whose profits last year reached $40,000,000. How was that money made? Before there was a union contract the company used prisoners from local jails to pick their grapes at the glorious price of seventy-five cents a day! They then imported workers from Mexico and Portugal at an average wage in 1972 of seventy-seven cents an hour. When the company signed up with the Teamsters in 1973 (instead of the Farm Workers which held contracts since 1967) and the pickers went on strike, the company had sixty of them put in jail. I say that is an atrocity.

*   *   *   *   *

Do you think it possible for peopl elike Cesar Chavez to succeed?

Mr. Nicholas Kisburg: I doubt it. I do not think he has the numbers or will have. Any time a union leader has to go to the consumer for help, he is in trouble. There are hundreds of organizational situations in which the workers never stand still long enough to be counted. Neither the National nor State Labor Relations

Board is going to help because an employer has forty ways, including postponements and appeals, to keep moving workers from voting. At some point the migrant has to go home perhaps hundreds of miles away. If a union leader really has the members in the field he strikes in the field and production stops. If the members continue to work, they are being terrorized or they are no longer fighting members. In either case the fighting union is dead.

*   *   *   *   *

What can the Church do that might be special?

Mrs. Dolores Huerta: Listen to poor people, who know what they need. And if they get good leadership from the Church, they are not likely to be sitting around crying about how bad things are. One of the sad things about recent poverty organizations was that time was spent sitting around bemoaning how badly they were treated by the system. The groups which do effective work sit around only to discuss how things can be improved and changed. If one answer fails, they move to try something else. A listening Church can be very helpful.

*   *   *   *   *

ABOUT THE CHURCH

Is the Church really afraid to take on those who commit injustice?

Mrs. Dolores Huerta: Even though the big Church provides support for poor men's causes, local priests are frequently scared to death to support those same causes because they will lose parishioners and contributions. The poor man has no difficulty in recognizing the difference between good and evil because he lives at the level of sheer survival. Because he is not dealing with his own survival, the priest develops objectivity, he weighs all the factors, and concludes that there is good and evil on both sides. So he loses the ability to say to a man of power: "What you are doing is evil."

If it is hard for the Church to take precise moral stands, what hope is there for the rest of the country? How can the Church be neutral when innocent people go hungry, some being killed? Such neutrality is wrong. This is especially true when you see the might amassed against the poor in a given fight, not only powerful economic and political combines, but even mighty trade unions.

*   *   *   *   *

What is the value of religious on a picket line?

Mrs. Dolores Huerta: Many people do not like to picket. Others say that religious especially should not be on a picket line. But a picket line is really a pilgrimage. When you walk up and down in front of a store you walk for justice. When you walk for justice in a big city, think of the farmer who has to walk hundreds of miles to feed you in very hot and very cold weather. A picket line is prayer in motion—praying that people will do something helpful, like not buying that lettuce, or grapes, or wine that comes to your table because someone else has literally sweat blood to get it there.

When people feel discrimination and oppression they acquire a scar which never goes away, even if the pain is replaced by numbness. It takes a baptism of fire to cauterize those wounds and some of the abuse heaped on Christ in his march up the hill of Calvary. That is why religious ought to be on picket lines.

*   *   *   *   *

Can the Church give more than it does to poor causes?

Msgr. George Kelly: It is always possible to do more. No one can give an accurate picture of the annual income of the 18,000 parishes functioning throughout all of the fifty states. A parish income in a given year might reach upwards toward the $1,000,000 mark, if it were a cathedral or a business parish in a large city, or struggle along with as little as $10,000 which in practice means poverty level.

The Church can always sell unused or unuseful properties and where possible that should always be done. This is not always as easy as it sounds. No one may want the property or the price offered is far below value. Or more frequently in changing cities, extreme caution must be exercised lest disposal of property—such as Church, rectory, and school—may prove to be a disaster in a following generation which seeks in the same neighborhood facilities which no longer exist, except at outrageous and impossible prices.

As far as parish income is concerned, between a fourth and a third of all current income is presently assigned to non-parochial causes, most of which have to do with the poor somewhere somehow. If one assumes for the sake of starting discussion that the average parish grosses $50,000 in a given year, then all American parishes together raise $900,000,000, of which a third goes to all kinds of other causes. Presuming that this income could be raised 5 percent next year, the effect is that $50,000,000 of new money is available, supposedly for the poor. This is a lot of money in gross numbers. But it would add only two dollars a year to the annual income of the American poor or finance only one-third of the cost of giving special education to the disadvantaged children in a city like New York.

Msgr. George Higgins likes to remind everyone quite correctly that this is the era of big money. He recalls that the last strike of the automobile workers cost the union in the neighborhood of $150,000,000 and to survive the union had to borrow money from the automotive corporations.

CHAPTER TEN

WHERE DO WE GO FROM HERE?

"We live at a time in the Church when our values are immensely confused. Those who do not want the bishop to tell them what to do in bed, want him to tell everyone what they should or should not be putting on the table. The pastor should let the parish council run the parish, but he should tell their children that daddy is a corporate bandit and mommy is a conspicuous consumer.

Councilmen against poverty meet until early morn deciding how to open up career ladders for Blacks, only to find themselves going home on the subway with elderly, immigrant ladies who, after cleaning the city's offices, exchange gossip about the sons they put through professional school. The young curate, known throughout the diocese for his eloquence about the needs of his people, when called about ten jobs for school dropouts, doesn't know the names of four kids. This is all very distressing."

MSGR. JOHN B. AHERN
Director of Family & Community Services
Catholic Charities
New York City

All that needs to be said about the Catholic Church and the American Poor has been said a thousand times. The plethora of Church documents, seminars, and sermons the world over would fill a new Vatican library, yet the problem remains a problem. That in itself tells us something. Poverty does not go away easily. Catholics do not solve it alone. On the basis of the historical record few can predict its final end this side of final judgment. However, this need not be the end of the world, except for those evolutionaries who, believing that the human condition always must get better and better, think the millennium of a modern Sybaris will be reached only by radical and violent action. It should be clear by now that if no one has come with the infallible answer, the solution is not at hand. Slide rules, whether used by experts at a *Bucharest Population Conference* or a *World Food Conference* in Rome, are not going to work. People themselves keep getting in the way of answers. They want babies the experts say they should not have. Or they spurn the tasteless food which nutritionists assert contains the balanced amount of protein and carbohydrates. Social reform, therefore, must be understood as more than the restructure of systems.

If the Church does not have all the answers, neither has government. That the poor of one kind or another will be always with us must be accepted as a fact of life. No single institution is going to change that fact. Together, institutions can improve conditions gradually and as they move along ease the burden of someone's poverty. Perhaps in expecting less, there will be less disappointment, and that in itself will be a blessing. Sometimes human beings who go hungry every day are made more miserable because false hopes are constantly raised by international delegates sipping cocktails in the plush hotels in Europe and the Third World. These conventioneers will still be talking about long-range programs as much in the year 2000 A.D. as they do today.[1]

Is this an unchristian pessimism? Not at all, because poverty as a general condition of mankind is not increasing. Standards of living are rising all over the world. Even backward nations are riding a powerful tide of economic growth. There is reasonable expectation that "income poverty"—enough resources in the hands of people to meet basic needs—will almost disappear in the course of this century. There will still be "poor people" by someone's standards—those not having enough education, health services, or work satisfactions. But these are inequalities which society can live with, even if many individuals cannot.

Perhaps the one serious problem still existing in the twenty-first century will be a state of mind among moulders of public opinion which insists on making human distress an everlasting hopeless condition. Robert Lampman describes this mental condition:

> Some writers have elected to portray the poverty problem in such a way as to convey a feeling of hopelessness. They refer to poor people as rejected, cast off, down trodden, forgotten and trapped in a vicious cycle of poverty breeding poverty. They allege that certain processes are cumulative, so that the poor are getting poorer, the immiseration of the proletariat is accelerating, and the poverty problem is swelling like some ugly cancerous growth. This method of characterization is a compound of Old Testament prophecy, Marxian economics, and gospel meeting eschatology. Poverty, it is said, is the work of national if not original sin; it will lead to, even if it will not be cured by, the downfall of capitalism or a religious or moral crisis. These writers assert that increasing deprivation indicates that existing remedies have all failed and that we need cataclysmic change in all social arrangements.[2]

Lampman calls this "amusing nonsense." First of all, more people are working on food distribution, technological development, investment in the Third World than ever before in history. Secondly, waiting in line at an American supermarket in any ghetto offers *prima facie* evidence of how well the American poor eat. This is not the end of the matter, nor ought it to be, but it is ten thousand leagues above the bottom line of the sea of poverty.

Obviously any sensible program which hopes to deal effectively with such a complicated subject begins with a working definition. Are we dealing with poverty? Or are we dealing with people of low income? The two are not the same. Indeed there are those who assert that poverty has nothing to do with income. As long ago as 1883, one of the early American sociologists, William Graham Sumner of Yale, claimed that the concept of a "poor man" was so elastic that it could only be defined in terms of the going mores. Lack of income is relative to people and cultures. So are the other ingredients associated with some pre-determined poverty level. By present day American standards most of the several billions of people who ever lived, and most of those who live now, have been and are poor. The American poor are part of that six percent of the world's population which produces and consumes over one-third of the world's output of goods and services, whose income level is at least twice that of Europe, ten times as high as that of Asia.[3] (And incidentally feeds four times as many people outside its borders than within.) Definitions of poverty, therefore, can be made to suit political, not socio-economic or cultural purposes. In the earlier days of Charles Booth, Sidney Webb, and Jacob Riis, poverty meant pauperism. Later it meant unstable employment and insufficient income. Now it covers lower class standing or lower social status. The poor man now is one who says he is poor or whom people call poor.

The Church comes to this problem speaking more of poor people than poverty, more of justice, discrimination, rights, family, education than mere lack of money. *Mater et Magistra* (1961) as much as *Rerum Novarum* (1891) defined the problem in these terms, as did Vatican II's *Pastoral Constitution on the Church in the Modern World*. The 1971 Roman Synod, in a published document entitled *Justice in the World*, defined the issue mainly in terms of justice and charity.[4]

When the Church talks about the poor she has a variety of objectives in mind. Paul VI in *Progressio Populorum* made human dignity his first concern. He supported men's legitimate striving

"to exercise greater personal responsibility to do more, learn more, and have more so that they might increase their personal worth."[5]

The emphasis is not on more money or on things that money can buy but on ways and means of affording men opportunity and skill to become better men. His immediate predecessor, John XXIII, warned Catholics to anticipate progress in modest terms. He asked them not to wear each other out with interminable arguments over which is the better way to social development because then the possible would never get done.[6]

Where, then, does the Church want Catholics to go? Over and above alleviating the pain of those living poorly, there are two general directions offered to men of faith—one of learning, one of action. First, Catholics, who hold a wide variety of political positions, must acquire knowledge of those insights and priorities which flow out of the gospel and the Christian tradition. Secondly, they must bring these insights and priorities to their own secular sphere of influence.[7]

The list of insights and priorities, like the Commandments, may total ten or two, depending on the mountain from which they are declared. Those who aspire to go about the Father's business in the world of political economy, might consider some or perhaps all of the following admonitions:

1. *Do not adore false social gods.*

This is as good a place as any to begin a list, if only because Moses and Christ both started their lists of "musts" with God. False gods in this context are those "doctrinal tenets which, at their roots or in their main points, are inconsistent with the Christian faith and its notion of man."[8] Popes consistently take this temptation seriously because they realize that people tend to follow the thinking of their earthly peer group, their class, nation, or culture, not their Popes.

One false god is the classical liberal doctrine which "claims to exalt personal liberty by freeing it from any regulation, urging it on to seek only power and advantage and regarding social ties among men as the ready result of spontaneous private initiatives."[9] This was the creed of robber barons. They abused freedom so much that their power to run their own business was ultimately curtailed. Few businessmen or trade union leaders believe anymore that the freedom to invest, manage, work, bargain collectively, or strike, is an unlimited right. A variety of social constraints are now accepted by all wielders of economic power.

Yet, classic liberalism, though dead, is not fully buried. The New Left now calls upon the same principle to justify the rude unseating of political, corporate, or ecclesiastical oppressors. Allegedly, the pursuit of social justice knows no moral right. Even violence can be exculpated because the cause itself is deemed right. The word "liberal" is given a Marxist meaning, viz, bread by which alone man lives must be obtained for the poor by any price. And so again do left and right join forces, as they always do, in asserting that business is business, "my" business is right, "yours" has no objective right to exist. A quarter of a century ago Fulton Sheen diagrammed the process by which this wedding is celebrated:

> "The liberal of the last generation invoked liberalism to free economic activity from state control; the liberal of today invokes liberalism to extend state control of the economic order. The old liberal was a defender of capitalism; the new liberal is reacting against capitalism and wants some form of collectivism or state control. The old liberal wanted liberty of press, speech and conscience within the framework of democracy; the new liberalism, reacting against the old liberalism, wants the liberty without the framework as its safeguard. The old liberal rebelled against taxation without responsibility; the new liberal wants the taxation as a handout without responsibility."[10]

There is some fascination in observing the popularity of the Marxist world in a country whose founding fathers were men of property. "Marx's love of the abstraction 'humanity,' his polemics against Utopian socialists for expecting morality to promote social improvement, his equation of natural rights with usurped middle class power, his disdain of respectability, personal profit, and freedom, except on behalf of the proletariat, are now commonplace concepts among the intellectuals of American social reform movements, even among Catholics who traditionally have been most wary of the allurement of Marxism."[11]

Yet Catholics, no matter how smart, are destined to have difficulty reconciling the two gospels. For one thing, righteous anger in a Christian saint is a far cry from the clenched fist and violent roars of a Marxist revolutionary. Class warfare grows no wheat, neither does it save a soul, and may destroy both. For another thing, the Marxist system, no matter who its bosses happen to be, tends to become a Garden of Eden with locked gates. Basic political freedoms do not exist. The quality of the bread is inferior, if there is bread at all. And the Bread of Life is a commodity rarely dispensed without great sacrifice. The Christian reformer by definition starts from and ends in a different place. In the process of achieving his goals even suffering and frustration have meaning.

Another false god who attracts Christians in our time is the professional economist, the trained student of government statistics who has a sure fire answer to high prices, high unemployment rates, tax distribution, the problems of developing nations. Except that his own philosophy of man and society makes him read data which is not there or just plain people knock his predictions into a cocked hat. Maybe this will be a president of the country who borrows to pay his bills and leaves to his successor the job of raising taxes and dealing with inflation. Or it may be conspirators in the houses of labor and management who raise wages and prices far beyond the levels justified by productivity. Or, foreign nations pursuing their own self interest for a change by refusing to buy American goods, and the perennial act of God following the path of some eternal course, may upset the most carefully calculated theory. One company posted a sign on every wall of its plant which read: "The most careful planning can never match dumb luck."

The Christian can enjoy his luck with the best of them. But he also has a sense of Providence. The Portuguese tradition which believes that "Every newborn child comes into the world with a loaf of bread under its arm" cannot be documented for every case. But it is that faith which forces the Christian to discern the presence of the True God and keeps him from falling down before newer models of the Golden Calf.

2. Do not make the social gospel vain and empty.

The social gospel of the Church, since it is of recent development, is always stated cautiously. There are so many different social arrangements, definitions of social injustice, and degrees of moral virtue and vice in the reformers themselves, that even Popes write about these questions as if they were dancing on hot coals.

It is much easier to determine the rightness and wrongness of adultery and what to do about it than to propose judgment and courses of action to the mayor of a city who must determine which category of employees in the interest of solvency should be fired first. Once Pope Paul VI seemed to justify revolution against "long-standing tyranny" only to back away a year later from the implication saying that a call to revolution was "far from our thought and language."[12]

But caution in expression is not to be interpreted as a denial of substance to that gospel. Historically the Church has assigned special significance to elements of gospel teaching because those elements become important to its very life and function. In the days of Peter and Paul emperor-worship, dispensing a few grains of incense before a Roman idol, was interpreted as no mere act of patriotism but a failure in faith. As such the penitential discipline was somewhat rough on compromisers. We do not worry about emperors or presidents today and saluting the flag or bearing arms has become quite virtuous. Later on going to Mass, making one's Easter Duty, being married by the priest became essential for the inner-life of Catholics, and they still are. But now the works of social justice have moved up to the center of the Catholic stage. Taking care of the poor and reorganizing society to make that easier is now a major work of the Church. Not every Christian is going to make his fidelity to Christ hinge on his heeding the social commandments, anymore than some very fine Catholics had a consistently even record on Mass attendance. But the "organized Church," that nemesis of individualists, has made the kind of decision characteristic of her operation from Jerusalem, through Nicea, Chalcedon, and Trent. The Church—officially through its bishops—has said that the work of justice is an essential modern day work for the Christian community.

The bishops assembled for the Roman Synod in 1971 stated the new requirements rather formally:

"Action on behalf of justice and participation in the transformation of the world fully appears to us as a constitutive dimension of the preaching of the Gospel, or, in other words, of the

Church's mission for the redemption of the human race and its liberation from every oppressive situation."[13]

In simple terms this means that the Church wants the contemporary Christian to go to Mass, confess his sins, be married by the priest *and* work for the remedy of conditions which oppress poor people. Hence, the Catholic conscience must be formed on social issues with the same sensitivity as the Church once formed its people on personal relationships, sexual morals, and loyalty to the Church.

Perhaps the words "sensitivity" and "conscience" are the key words. Catholics, apart from the criticism leveled against them by their own malcontents, always had a firm grasp of special sensitivities and a formed conscience about certain rights and wrongs. Dispensing kindness and goods to the poor has been a notable Catholic virtue and its absence a subject of many confessional conversations. But now the Church wants Catholics to help the poor grab hold of their own situation and assert their rights—with the support of Catholics! And if better-off Catholics are not so inclined, the Church is perfectly willing to have them feel guilty—at a time when that word is not considered sanitary.

As a matter of fact middle-class Catholics, who far from being a despicable tribe to be treated contemptuously, are a remarkable lot of faithful Christians, who by numbers alone and properly engaged could change the face of their own country. They have little reason perhaps to empathize with the American poor, who in their view will make it as their own fathers and mothers made it. But they also ought to know how far bishops are willing to go in pushing them to the ultimate of their Christian commitment. American bishops are as conscious of American prosperity as the laity. But Brazilian bishops state for a continent what American bishops might state for an area—with the expectation that Catholic Americans might take the directive seriously:

The moment a system fails to provide for the common good and shows favor to a particular few, the Church has the duty not only to denounce the injustice, but also to cut free from that unjust system, seeking to collaborate with some other system more just and likely to meet the necessity of the times . . .

Christians and their pastors should learn to see the hand of the Almighty in the events that, periodically, put down the mighty from their seats and exalt the humble, or send away the rich with empty hands and fill the hungry.[14]

These judgments and decisions involve tough discernment. They do not carry universal agreement and require from Christians soundness in the assessment of facts and possibilities. But the social objectives are neither vain nor inane but at the heart of Catholic Christianity as defined by those empowered to define them.

3. *Keep holy the laws of life.*

The Catholic Church may be the only world-wide institution which thinks there are laws of life at all and that they are holy, i.e., they pertain to God and man's final salvation. The contemporary thinking world judges law, like truth itself, to be man-made, not God-given. Within this latter context powerful men impose their will and their truth upon weaker men. For the generality of men, therefore, salvation in this world must depend on the wide popular use of freedom. The power usually possessed only by the strong can be acquired by the weak through the skillful use of superior numbers. Freedom, therefore, is the first article of faith and democracy is its church.

No American, least of all Catholic Americans, would deny the beneficient results which have come to their own country because ultimate political power is in the hands of the people, because there is a viable political machinery by which people make their value choices known. David J. O'Brien, historian, declared in an address to the 1974 National Conference of Catholic Charities in Boston, that this freedom is more important today than ever. He based this judgment on the sanctions given to freedom by the Church herself:

In America power as freedom, the power of ordinary men and women to make choices and act upon them, must replace power as control, the ability of some people to control and manipulate others. The American revolution is the ongoing struggle to empower people to take on responsibility for their own lives and for the life of the community. It is a revolution which welcomes the surging demands of minorities, of women, of the young and the poor, to take responsibilities of self-determination, seeing in such movements vital new energy for the ongoing revolutionary struggle.[15]

O'Brien further concludes that it is not necessary for Christians to agree on politics; it is necessary that they choose because choices tend to limit arbitrary power which can be legitimated only through "mechanisms of consent."[16]

The case for political democracy is very well stated here and as a plea for greater citizen participation is quite relevant to the needs of these times. But as a meaningful contribution to the problems of poverty some addition and completion is needed. Freedom as an abstract concept is useful to Laissez-Faire Democrats and Marxist Socialists. In the one case, freedom favors those better able to use its power. In the latter case freedom favors those who have the votes. In neither case is freedom tied to anything but power, the power to do something for oneself, to be a capitalist or a proletarian, a White majority or a Black minority. In this sense freedom is still free enterprise—a game of playing, sometimes by upper class, sometimes by lower class. Freedom, standing alone, does not achieve justice in government anymore than it did in business.

One of the reasons why "freedom" or "democracy" cannot be a nostrum for the poor is that the process will always go against them, even if they succeed in what O'Brien calls the "ongoing revolutionary struggle." There is probably more participation in government today than at any other time in American history. In yesterday's politics one could count only on involvement by corporations, trade unions, or farm bureaus in national government, and ethnic groups in local government. Within the last two decades we have witnessed the rise of scientists, educators, intelligentsia, Black, youth, and poor, all playing what Daniel Bell calls "a role in the game of resource allocation."[17] This increase in participation by larger numbers of groups each seeking diverse or competing ends paradoxically ends up in paralysis of government. In the absence of a sense of right or of groups governed by reason democratic consensus becomes impossible. Without consensus only naked power remains—the votes of those most amenable to purchase by one political party or the other. This always means conflict. Unquestionably there are always social actors who wish to see society torn apart by persistent conflict but they ought not be Christian. The end result of that warfare is repression of one sizeable force or another. This has little to do with justice of which the Church speaks.

In the economic arena the freedom-absolute can be harmful mostly to the people for whom it is offered as a nostrum. It is almost a law of life that economic self-interest is a more powerful motivating force than political self-interest. Self-serving economic choices by the majority will always bring harm to the poor, and here the majority are working men not economic royalists. People will always vote their priorities and those include very few strangers. No politician who needs re-election will tell people they will be taxed more; no union leader will recommend a smaller wage increase for a cause unrelated to their own pressing needs. Neither politician nor union leader would ever again be re-elected. What citizens under normal conditions surrender their livelihood so that some others can have a livelihood? American workers, exercising their freedom, took jobs away from British workers. Now German, Japanese, even Arabian workers, are taking jobs away from Americans on the principle that in the game of making a living all is fair. The freedom-absolute applied across the board to wage rates, for example, only increases differentials, adds to total costs, overpricing and ultimately to unemployment.

American Catholics have always taken their democracy seriously but have never quite bought the freedom-absolute which guarantees jobs in the federal government to active Communists and in Catholic universities to heretics. Their fathers lived through the tyranny of maxi-mobs, and they watch now the disintegration of their national and religious institutions at the hands of mini-mobs. The common Catholic folk have a solid understanding that Catholic social thought about care of the poor, about government economic programs, about democratic processes is really an organic body of truth. When a single item—even the sacred gift of human freedom—is isolated or inflated, the end result is human degradation. Intellectuals on the contrary see the difficulty of absolutizing "public order," even while bestowing on "freedom" an explosive quality. Pope Paul recently has taken note of this tendency in the Catholic world. He warned:

> One must not use, or rather abuse, an isolated truth contained in the great framework of Christian wisdom, without taking into account the other truths connected with it. Otherwise the result will be lack of balance and a one-sided system.[18]

Popes understand, better than most, that to place freedom in focus is to expose themselves to the charge of being "repressive and reactionary, exclusively authoritarian and anti-democratic." Paul VI bluntly asserts that to talk about freedom is impossible if one does not also simultaneously include the "built-in aspects of freedom, namely its intrinsic relation with moral obligation."[19] Mistaken choices can be dangerous and oppressive for a national community. If choices are not related to truth or to law, they must be made for reasons of passion, selfish interest, lack of will power, fear, opportunism, or conformism. If choices are not informed choices nor related to the right nor to the moral nor to the lawful, they must be related to misinformation and to the wrong, the immoral, and to the illegal. On the latter basis, the politics of choosing ultimately means someone's force which begets someone else's counterforce. And no one should believe that this conflict represents the full expression of human freedom.

Majority vote is a useful instrument for deciding political questions, especially when people cannot agree on values. But majority vote does not always make right. When the poor are concerned, it rarely does. Popes, parents, presidents, bankers, union officials and John Doe too must learn to know how to respond to rightness, even though the world is against them. Otherwise Whites will keep themselves far removed from Blacks and Blacks will develop reverse-nationalism. Trade union leaders and entrepreneurs in our society continue to pursue their own profit, politicians declare injustice to be justice because their constituents make those decisions the name of the game.

Marxists are smarter than Christians. They tend to emphasize structures and limit reform to tactical alterations in existing situations. The Church goes further. She says that structural changes will never do, unless those structures relate to values other than people's will or people power. These values are the natural laws of living, the same principles which underpinned John Courtney Murray's concept of the civil or civilized society.

4. *Honor the Christian Tradition.*

Advantage ought always to be taken of the patrimony bequeathed by tradition. Catholics are as forgetful as anyone else, but they ought to realize that their Church possesses the single largest privately owned health, welfare, education, parish, social action system in the entire world. The only available medical service in dozens of American counties is to be found in Catholic hospitals. The Catholic record in social legislation, labor law, in welfare law, in social security law, in housing law is unexcelled. The Church may in fact lose this patrimony because today almost alone she stands relatively independent of hyper-organized government. The public bureaucracy has begun to look upon voluntary effort as a licensed function of government, rather than the independent effort of citizens to provide service, if not apart from government, at least in collaboration. To belittle one of the few private social forces for good left in the country does not indicate good sense.

The Church itself is not immune to the *evangelium* called secularization. There are *agents provocateurs* in high Church roles who accept this as the inevitable condition of being modern. On the other hand, most leaders of the Church see secularity as a new opportunity to demonstrate again the value of the faith, not as once it did in tents and catacombs, but from the strength of its own accumulated resources of people, of services, of schools, of agencies, of buildings. Let others advise the sale of holy oils with the price to be given to the poor, but those paltry sums will never help the poor, even if they amounted to millions. Chatter about fighting the structures of the Church or its leaders or its influence is usually the cant of the Church's enemies, who wish to bring the Church down. Such people rarely make an examination of conscience about their own motives, faith, or competence but in spite of them the Catholic tradition goes on.

5. Do Not Kill Initiative.

Too many members of the Church, even critics, wait for a Papal directive before they engage in responsible efforts on behalf of the poor. If their programs are good they will acquire a permanent role in the ongoing Church structure. If they are not, they will serve a temporary purpose and die. No one ever really prevents the committed Christian from doing his good thing, not even the alleged bogeymen of another day, Francis J. Spellman or Francis A. McIntyre. Ecclesiastics have their own points of view, they approve and disapprove, they move with or against some person or some activity for anyone of a dozen reasons. The real reforming persons with ingenuity, sanity, and a sense of the Church, generally have their way. Ask Dorothy Day.

Harebrained and even violent schemes sometimes seek prior and ongoing blessing from the bishop. No bishop in his right mind is so senseless as to sign a blank check. The more important fact is that the Church does not stand in the way of many good things, even though she disapproves a few. Within the Church there are a few *imprimaturs* and many *nihil obstats*.

Pope Paul stated the case rightly in *Progressio Populorum*.

While the Hierarchy has the role of teaching and authoritatively interpreting moral laws and precepts that apply in this matter, the laity have the duty of using their own initiative and taking action in this area without waiting passively for directives and precepts from others. They must try to infuse a Christian spirit into people's mental outlook and daily behavior, into the laws and structures of the civil community.[20]

Popes and bishops can only hope that emerging laymen come out as Christian spokesmen and not merely voices for their own class or peer group. These are hopes only which no hierarch can monitor. The hierarchs can talk about the tradition but only people live it and love it.

6. Do Not Profane The Poor But Make Them Faithful.

The respectful person is the one who takes a second look at another. He discovers by that go around a quality which did not seem so attractive at first sight. Because the poor are different, they deserve a second look. The same blood runs through their veins and the same ambitions. St. Vincent de Paul did not provide handouts to professional beggars, but would not allow the French King to incarcerate them because that violated a saint's sense of their dignity. The poor can be as contemptible as some rich, and if they are part of a mob, just as arrogant. So they need a second look, which is what respect is all about.

But how can they be made faithful? Part of the process has to do with looking them in the eye without sympathy but with a readiness to help. The other part is to know their spokesmen. The poor suffer more from their spokesmen than from their condition. Like every one they need help of two friends, one to talk about their cause, the other to talk about their conduct. Probably, the only reason the Irish eventually were civilized came as a result of priests fighting on their side, while their bishops excommunicated the worst of their leaders to keep the rest honest. We listen usually to those who make us comfortable, never to those who improve us, which probably explains why mothers are so important to the young. But the poor, while their cause is being fought, have to be told, scolded if necessary, about the importance of virtue, good habits, and the importance of work.

7. Leave the Work to the Laity.

A new kind of clericalism is abroad in the land today which seems to suggest that by the nature of the new understanding of their calling priests make good congressmen, good poverty leaders, and if need be good revolutionaries. The argument goes something like this: Religious commitment in our times means acceptance of political action for justice's sake. The priest is the religious professional. Ergo, he is or ought to be a political activist. We are not talking here of the priest who becomes poor himself or whose life style is consonant with the living condition of the people he serves; nor do we mean the priest who uses his pulpit or a lecture hall to speak out on behalf of the poor. These ministries have an old and distinguished position in the Church and relate to politics only indirectly. When the new clericalists speak of political action for priests and religious, they mean involvement in the political rumble, campaigning for votes, choosing up sides, drafting legislation, upsetting institutions and holding political office.[21]

It should be clearly understood that the Church has never made the exclusion of priests from practical politics a Catholic absolute. There is a proper role for a priest in public affairs, and many priests, and not a few bishops, have been good preachers of a political gospel and good/bad counsellors to the politicians out there on the firing line. But as a general rule the Church does not want priests giving, or seeming to give, official sanction to what for the most part will always be one partisan choice over another; nor does she relish the spectacle of priests fighting their own parishioners, even their own fellow priests. Because political priests from Cardinal Wolsey to Father Coughlin have betrayed or compromised the Church, the popes of the past century have excluded direct priestly intervention as a proper clerical role.

Richard McCormick quotes the Chilean Bishops' response to eighty of their political-minded priests: "The political choice of the priest, if—as in this case—it is presented as a logical and ineluctable consequence of his Christian faith, implicitly condemns every other option and constitutes a blow to the liberty

of other Christians."[22] Gary Wills, who was right wing before he
became left wing, rejected such clerical authority because it

> tends to make the layman superfluous for articulating informed
> Catholic response to any technical challenge of the age.[23]

Quite oppositely the Church has ordained the laity, not priests,
as chief ministers for the work of saving the world. Only a few
years ago Paul VI reaffirmed this teaching:

> While the hierarchy has the role of teaching and authorita-
> tively interpreting the moral laws that apply in this matter,
> the laity have the duty of using their own initiative and taking
> action in this area without waiting passively for directives and
> precepts.[24]

The difficulties experienced by the Church with worker-priests
in France is clear evidence that neither the Church nor the poor
are served well by overdominating priests, priests who talk and
act like political ward heelers, many of whom later give up the
priesthood and the Church. A quarter century ago, one of the
vibrant social action movements of the American Church was the
Association of Catholic Trade Unionists, a laymen's apostolate
sustained by the energy of countless priests. Fr. John Cronin
probably concludes rightly that interest in the Church's social
teaching and, a fortiori, movements like ACTU, declined during
the 1950's "because we believed that poverty was becoming only
a matter of history in this prosperous nation."[25] But priests bat-
tling publicly over proper organizational and political procedures
were not very helpful to apostolic laymen. Priests tend to be
absolutizers. Even when they argue for pluralism they argue absolutely. In the ACTU case, the New York and Detroit chapters
differed in approach from those in Chicago and Pittsburgh but the
decline of the entire movement was not stemmed by the activities
of debating priests, including this writer.[26]

The *Christian Family Movement,* launched in 1947 by Msgr.
Reynold Hillenbrand of Chicago, came closer to being an ideal

social action training program for the priests and laity of the United States. At one point at least 50,000 married couples across the American continent working in at least 100 dioceses made up an impressive cadre of enthusiastic evangelists for the Catholic social gospel. Apart from the difficulty of married couples with large families really accomplishing significant social reform, CFM was in many ways a better vehicle of Catholic involvement than the Confraternity of Christian Doctrine. However, the body of bishops never quite saw the significance of that movement, which regretfully remained detached from the mainstream of the Church. Some of its leadership later fell prey to the allurements of contraception, membership declined, and CFM ultimately ceased being an effective Catholic activity. But in the wake of Vatican II, which one might have expected to result otherwise, a great opportunity was lost to energize nationally a lay apostolate, one which the Church still urgently needs. This, however, was not the first such Catholic misadventure. By the time CFM was beginning to attract priests and couples, John Cronin was reporting that sixty-five Catholic social action centers existed in forty-three major cities promoting trade unionism, social legislation, welfare programs, hardly any of which exist any more.[27]

But now that the Church leaders themselves have come around to requiring a lay apostolate working to bring justice to the poor, no lay apostolate of any significance seems to be visible. What ignored groups like ACTU and CFM once did well Pope John said now must be done more than ever.

> Education to act in a Christian manner in economic and social matters will hardly succeed, in our opinion, unless those being educated play an active role in their own formation, and unless formal instruction is supplemented by activity undertaken for the sake of gaining experience.[28]

Rebuilding movements of this genre will not be easy for a Church torn apart by dissent and wearied by disillusionment. Yet if social action be the goal, the priests are goal tenders, nothing more. The offensive and defensive lines and backs are laymen,

whose whole life is in, by and of the world. Fifty thousand ordained preachers will not save the world, but the right 50,000,000
laymen just might.

   8. *Let the priests talk for God first, to their faithful second,
and then to the world.*

The in-word is "prophet," usually understood these days
as meaning the man who "denounces injustice wherever it appears."[29] The only trouble with that phrasing is that it ignores
the very meaning of the term itself. Etymologically, the prophet
is "a man who speaks for God." The discovery that Christ "stirred
up" the Jews has led some commentators to call him an "agitator"
—and to imply that his major and exclusive thrust was against
the Jewish *status quo,* and not for the "good news" which dominates his gospel. It is not surprising, therefore, in the present mood
of the Church that the popular prophet has become the purveyor
of "bad news." This was not always so, nor does this revolutionary
interpretation do justice to the meaning of priest-prophet.

   The priest-prophet is truly the man chosen from among men
to be their representative before God, to offer gifts and sacrifices,
but also to teach. Seemingly as far back as the early days of the
Church priests have had again and again to be reminded what
their basic role was. In the first century of the Church the author
of the Epistle to the Hebrews remonstrated with priests:

> You have become deaf. Although by this time you should be
> teaching others, you need to have someone teaching you again
> the basic elements of the oracles of God.[30]

And the learning process for friends can only begin with the
Church itself. Edward Schillebeeckx indicates that the Church has
a great deal to learn from the world,[31] which is true enough, but
priests better learn in depth what after two thousand years the
Church has to say about their role, lest they be swallowed up by
that world, as a child sometimes is ensnared by a worldly-wise
teacher. Furthermore, not enough attention is paid today to the

spiritual qualifications of the priest who would prophesy on behalf of the world. There is a secular bias against judging the
worthiness of a cause by the personal worthiness of its promoter.
This disconnection is probably a pragmatic basis for evaluating
projects in a society which has little interest in spiritula qualifications. But not so for the Church, nor for anyone who would claim
to speak for God. A scrutiny of motivations, piety, and principles is always in order among those engaged in Christ's work.
The holiness of life in a Christian reformer is always one indica-
tion of God's blessing. Unfortunately, in cigar-filled and sometimes
Scotch-filled hotel rooms where the future of some special Catholic
work is under discussion, little reference is made to this side of the
question.

All of these considerations are apropos to programmatics of
human liberation from oppression. The priest, in this activity as
in anything else he does, comes as father to his family and shepherd to his flock. He is not a comrade nor a scholar placing himself
on a level with his friends. Friendly he ought to be, but like Christ
he is a priest there to teach, to rule, and to sanctify. In the field of
social action he is warned repeatedly by a succession of popes to
get laymen involved in the cure of social problems.[32] Pius XII was
even stronger than John XXIII, insisting a short time before he
died that priests have their own faithful undertake

> tasks that he can perform as well or even better than the priest
> and allow him to act freely and exercise personal responsibility
> within the limits set for his work or demanded by the common
> welfare of the Church.[33]

The first role of the priest is to motivate the right kind of laity
to become involved in the cause of social justice. Where are all
the social actionists usually to come from? From an institution,
parish or school, where priestly influence is high. If the wrong
kind of Catholics emerge the blame usually lies with some priest.
Dealing with intellectuals may call for priests who are somewhat
smart but they need not be as bright as they need to be holy.
However, problems between priests and lay activists usually are

unrelated to ordination or superordination, superiority or inferiority. They flow rather from a variety of vices which contaminate bad relationships of any kind—perhaps pride, arrogance, ambition, rash judgment, impatience, disregard or disobedience of simple moral imperatives.[34] However well Frederick Ozanam or Jacques Maritain might have served as spiritual directors for functionaries of social reconstruction, it is priests whose ordinary work this is. If they do this badly, the solution is to be sought in the better selection and training of priests for the work of priests, not in the usurpation of the work of Christian laymen.

Let the priest, if he will, walk the picket line in the midst of a watching world. Let him mount his pulpit or his platform on behalf of poor people. Let him encourage strikers and dissenters, if justice indicates that. Let him even work in private with laymen over some radically upsetting project. Let him become a thorn in the side of legislators and bureaucrats. Let him take any political action his common sense dictates as necessary to a good cause. But may he understand he is "a man who speaks for God," may he know what he is doing, may he do what secular thing he does because lay leaders are non-existent, may he have good judgment, the ability to know right from wrong, the humility to know when he is in over his head. And because the Church rides with the priest, as she does not ride with the layman, may he be worthy of his role and, above all, a man who talks to God and listens to Him before he talks for Him.

9. *Let the Bishops become leaders of the Catholic social action movement.*

Pre-Vatican II triumphalists always hope for an episcopal leadership which would wipe out the reformers and return the Church to sacristy chores. Post-Vatican II triumphalists look for bishops to live in tents and wear sandals on picket lines. The latter would even take more kindly to bishops if only they stopped talking about marriage and sex the Catholic way. It seems that no matter what bishops do these days they suffer, which is what the price of episcopacy was in the beginning. Running the Church as the apostles assuredly did is bound to draw a little of their blood. Certainly in troubled times the bishops ought to be out in front of their people with their voice and staff. When Catholic doctrine or life style is threatened they may not be silent, nor arbitrarily select their positions, nor worry about their image, nor hide behind scholars, certainly not behind public relations men. If the faithful are troubled in their faith about its meaning or content, the bishops above all must teach them, even if it means trouble for them. And if the highest authorities of the Church—Pope, Council, Synod—tell them that social doctrine and social action are central to contemporary evangelization, then the bishops ought to be out there in front too.

Someone ought to tell bishops that they are the heads of the Church. And to remind anyone else interested in hearing that Vatican II, far from deposing them, reaffirmed their core role as divinely created representatives for governing the Church. In recent years they look like caretakers, not overseers. By and large they have remained arm's length from the Church's social doctrine since 1891, but recently from other teaching manifestations as well. Many good episcopal statements on social problems have been issued periodically, beginning with the *Bishops' Program of Social Reconstruction,* written for them in 1919 by John A. Ryan. But within their own dioceses bishops did little to train priests and nuns, let alone laity, on social questions. And while generous with their *nihil obstats* to others, they did not make social action a major activity of their year-to-year administration. Common gossip explains this inaction by the conservatism of bishops, even though Andrew Greeley tells anyone who wants to listen that bishops are more progressive than priests, who are also ahead of their own parishioners on social matters. John F. Cronin tells the story that the 1958 statement of the American bishops on racial discrimination was actually strengthened by bishops designated by the press as conservative while "one extremely influential prelate widely classified as a liberal opposed its issuance" because it might be too hot a subject for the bishops' conference to handle.[35] However, if there is estrangement presently between bishops and social activists, this is due partly to a failure many years ago to root the movements for peace and justice in diocesan machinery, which is where the popes wanted it in the first place.[36] Now that the energy of some vital apostolic movements has been sapped by inattention, the bishops contemplate making "justice" a basic part of the forthcoming *National Catechetical Directory* and the diocesan office for justice and peace an important administrative arm of the Church.[37]

Although important, this will only be the beginning of the matter. Inclusion of a document on justice in the *Directory* to be used in schools and conferences hopefully will guarantee authentic instruction of the faithful. And if social service and social action are to be made co-equal ministries with the customary sacred and sacerdotal functions, it is quite clear that the bishops themselves, not delegates, must support and guarantee not only the authenticity but the implementation. Influence and leadership cannot stop with teaching. Bishops themselves must acquire a certain competence—like any public official—to decide how specific social interventions of the Church, many of which will be conflict situations, promote the good of the Church and the well-being of men. As much as politicians, they have to be at home with socio-economic experts and to develop their favorites. Today's social questions are quite complicated. In the first place, forty years of Keynesian economics, federally administered social welfare programs, international economic and military sorties against Communism have covered up some structural and moral weaknesses in our society. Beyond that, it is now commonly accepted that the economic policies of the federal government—liberal or conservative—are not the final answer to poverty. The federal bureaucracy now serves itself rather than the public, has become insensitive to local and regional opinion, has wasted vital resources and cost unnecessary billions of hard-earned dollars. The reform of the tax system, reduction of bureaucratic costs, balancing prices and wages, international economic cooperation may have more to do with the long-range well-being of the poor than skirmishes in dioceses between the have-nots and the have-only-a-little-mores. Bishops ought to know enough to evaluate their experts who, even though Catholic, may not be sympathetic to stated Catholic goals.

Within the Catholic community are those who have a pragmatic approach to economic solutions and those who would opt for a socialist government in this country.[38] Bishops ought to be sure of themselves in dealing with those experts, enough to realize when science has left the room and a hostile ideology has walked in.

While Hans Kung thinks that the central contemporary question for the Church is how to bring the stable structures of the Church into line with the need for greater community life among Catholics,[39] the bishops cannot sacrifice getting the required job done to generated we-feeling. Granted that bishops should be concerned with fraternity, good-will, and a flexibility of administration which encourages individual initiative, their main role is to promote the values inherent in the Christian commitment. In our time bishops have failed in their responsibilities not because they were uninformed, and not because they were evil men. In fact rarely have bishops been more intelligent and nicer people. They have failed because they have not held onto the strengths of the Church and have not dealt constructively with dissent and vulnerability.[40] Some bishops have been dreamers staying in the safe world of abstraction, e.g., "We must wait for the Pope" or "My job is to preach the gospel not solve human conflicts." Others still have been adventurers and opportunists who risked the moral reputation of the Church on some daring but untested gambles.

The role of the bishop is never easy. Winning consent calls for wisdom on his part and strength. He has to have a good sense of the Catholic essentials, as distinguished from the peripheral. Because in recent years they have compromised essentials and absolutized peripheral aspects of their office, their future functioning becomes more difficult. This is especially true now that the Church wants the bishops to take social questions under their wing, questions which the world, Catholic and non-Catholic, normally believes are outside their competence or authority.

But the introduction of bishops into an active role in the social movement will have some long-range benefits. First, it will make Catholics at least conscious of their social responsibilities and less resistant to sensible change. Secondly, it will guarantee that the Catholic doctrine is soundly stated. A line of demarcation between those who are with and those against the Church will be clearly drawn. Thirdly, priests and religious who work among the poor will be encouraged by episcopal support and will be glad to know they do not work alone. Fourthly, when practical judgments are involved, the creative bishop will represent the voice of sanity. He will—hopefully—neither be the captive of establishment nor of destructive change. He may put the whole weight of his diocese, though not necessarily all of his people, behind a strike or a boycott, or hopefully too condemn bad judgment and violence, whenever that course of action is indicated. Fifthly, because responsible leadership—i.e., which pays a high price for mistakes—does its homework, the chances are everyone else down the line will do so too. In the long-run the bishop can be a stabilizing, as well as a creative force, whose interventions will be respected, even when they are disapproved.

This is precisely what bishops are intended to be—respected leaders and functioning authorities. They need not always be personally involved. Sometimes on a major front they should be. That calls for prudent judgment. But their diocese ought to be involved from chancery officials, to teaching religious, to parish councils. Bishops cannot approve everything that goes on down the line. They may be called to disavow something going on in the name of Catholicity which is inimical to a people's cause or the Church itself. This is an important aspect of governance, one neglected in an era which has seen fraternal correction of bishops the common syndrome. But without such active bishops the promotion of peace and justice will remain merely an exercise in book-learning, nothing more.

10. *Let Christian apostles love their fellowman because they love Christ first.*

The 1974 Synod of Bishops spent the better part of two months discussing what bishops are all about, i.e., evangelization, making disciples of all nations. They decreed no final answers because bishops know that final answers are God's private property. But the assembled two hundred excellencies from every corner of the

Church talked mainly about praying to God and ministry to man, which is about where Christ came in. Some bishops thought the world needed more elevation of mind and heart to God, more meditation and contemplation about ultimate meaning and divine providence; other bishops associated modern evangelization with a new and vigorous social ministry. Obviously, within the Catholic tradition praying people should minister, and ministers if they be Christian should pray. Everyone will not be equally good at both, although the best Catholic leaders, those who set the tone for the rest, must pray well if they are to minister well.

The most important consideration, therefore, is that the dedicated Catholic social actionist be rooted in the Church for which he would speak. Basically he acts, if he acts apostolically, under the driving force of that faith which is Catholic in essence. Almost 125 years ago John Henry Newman reflected the right mood in any age for Catholic witnesses to the world.

What I desiderate in Catholics is the gift of bringing out what their religion is; it is one of those 'better gifts' of which the Apostle bids you be 'zealous.' You must not hide your talent in a napkin, or your light under a bushel. I want a laity, not arrogant, nor rash in speech, not disputatious, but men who know their religion, who enter into it, who know just where they stand, who know what they hold, and what they do not, who know their need so well, that they can give an account of it, who know so much of history that they can defend it . . . I have no apprehensions you will be the worse Catholics for familiarity with these subjects, provided you cherish a vivid sense of God above and keep in mind that you have souls to be judged and to be saved.[41]

NOTES FOR CHAPTER TEN

1 See Arthur McCormack, "Sticking to The Subject at Rome: Food," *America,* November 16, 1974, pp. 292-294.

2 Robert J. Lampman, *Ends and Means of Reducing Income Poverty,* (Chicago: Markham), p. 135.

3 *Ibid.,* p. 52.

4 This document is available in *The Pope Speaks,* vol. XVI, no. 4, p. 383 ff.

5 Paul VI, *Progressio Populorum,* (no. 6) in *The Pope Speaks,* vol. XII, no. 2 (1967), p. 146.

6 John XXIII, (nos. 236 ff) in *The Pope Speaks,* vol. VII, no. 4 (1962), pp. 338 ff.

7 Paul VI, "Octagesima Adveniens,",*The Pope Speaks,* vol. 16, no. 2, 1971, p. 162.

8 *Ibid.,* p. 150.

9 *Ibid.*

10 Fulton J. Sheen, *Communism and the Conscience of the West,* (New York: Doubleday, 1948), p. 19.

11 See Alvin W. Gouldner, *The Coming Crisis of Western Sociology,* (New York: Basic Books, 1970), pp. 405-406.

12 Paul VI, *Progressio Populorum,* no. 31 reads "A revolutionary uprising—save where there is manifest, longstanding tyranny which would do great damage to fundamental personal rights and dangerous harm to the common good of the country—produces new injustices, throws more elements out of balance, and brings on new disasters. A real evil should not be fought against at the cost of greater misery." A year later, March 27, 1968, in a general audience the Pope denied he supported a theology of revolution. What seems clear is that in those social circumstances revolution was understandable, but not accorded a prior benediction.

13 "Justice in the World," *The Pope Speaks,* vol. 16, no. 4, 1971.

14 Fifteen Bishops (from Brazil, Oceania, Yugoslavia, Lebanon, China, Laos), "A Message to the People of the Third World," July 31, 1967, in the *Catholic Mind,* January 1968, pp. 40-41.

15 David J. O'Brien, "The American Revolution: 1776-1976," *Origins,* vol. 4, no. 19, October 31, 1974, p. 301.

16 *Ibid.,* p. 303.

17 For an elaboration of this argument see an article by Daniel Bell and Virginia Held, "The Community Revolution," *The Public Interest,* no. 16, Summer, 1969.

18 Paul VI, An address titled "Freedom and Truth," *L'Osservatore Romano,* English Edition, July 18, 1974, p. 1.

19 *Ibid.*

20 Paul VI, *Progressio Populorum* in *The Pope Speaks,* vol. XII, no. 2 (1967), p. 170.

21 For a sympathetic view of priest involvement see Peter J. Henriot, S.J., "Social Sin and Conversion: A Theology of the Church's Social Involvement," *Chicago Studies,* vol. II (1972), pp. 115-130; and "Politics and the Priest," *Commonweal,* vol. 96 (1972), pp. 495-98.

22 See Richard J. McCormick, "The Socio-Political Mission of the Church," *Theological Studies,* vol. 34 (March, 1973), no. 1, p. 97.

23 Gary Wills, *op. cit.,* p. 44.

24 Paul VI, *Progressio Populorum,* in *Loc. cit.,* no. 81.

25 John F. Cronin, S.S., "Social Action: Myth or Reality?", *Catholic Mind,* December, 1967, p. 41.

26 George A. Kelly, "The ACTU and Its Critics," *Commonweal,* vol. XLIX, no. 12 (December 31, 1948), pp. 298-301. For the reaction of other priests see the issues of January 14th, 21st, 28th, 1949 in "Communications."

27 John F. Cronin, *Catholic Social Action,* (Milwaukee: Bruce, 1948), pp. 229-235.

28 John XXIII, *Mater et Magistra* (May 15, 1961), *loc. cit.,* nos. 85-86.

29 Richard J. McCormick, *loc. cit.,* p. 94.

30 Heb. 5: 11-12.

31 Edward Schillebeeckx, *World and Church,* (New York: Sheed and Ward, 1971), p. 112.

32 John XXIII, *Mater et Magistra, loc. cit.,* no. 232.

33 Pius XII, "Address to the Second Congress of the Lay Apostolate," October 5, 1957, (N.C.W.C. Editor), no. 20.

34 For a discussion of the "seven capital sins" which sometimes interfere with Christian social action, see George A. Kelly, *The Lay Apostle,* (Washington, D. C., N.C.W.C., 1963), pp. 19-20.

35 John F. Cronin, "Social Action: Myth or Reality?", *Catholic Mind,* December, 1967, p. 40.

36 *Papal Teachings on the Lay Apostolate, op. cit.,* nos. 88, 667, 848, 880, 915.

37 See J. Bryan Hehir, "The Ministry For Justice," in a newsletter called *Network Quarterly,* published by the U.S. Catholic Conference, vol. 2, no. 3, Summer, 1974.

38 Peter J. Henriot, S.J., "Is The System Reformable?", *Commonweal,* vol. CI, no. 10, December 20, 1974, p. 255.

39 Hans Kung, *The Council, Reform, and Reunion,* (New York, Sheed & Ward, 1967), p. 18.

40 For a good discussion of this general subject see Philip Selznick, *Leadership in Administration: A Sociological Interpretation,* (Evanston, Illinois: Row, Peterson, 1957).

41 John Henry Newman, *Lectures on the Present Position of Catholics in England,* (New York: Longmans, Green, 1913), p. 390.

INDEX

An Interesting Thought

The publication you have just finished reading is part of the apostolic efforts of the Society of St. Paul of the American Province. A small, unique group of priests and brothers, the members of the Society of St. Paul propose to bring the message of Christ to men through the communications media while living the religious life.

If you know of a young man who might be interested in learning more about our life and mission, ask him to contact the Vocation Office in care of ALBA HOUSE, at 2187 Victory Blvd., Staten Island, New York 10314. Full information will be sent without cost or obligation. You may be instrumental in helping a young man to find his vocation in life. *An interesting thought.*